HERITAGE
OF
IRELAND

HERITAGE
-OF-
IRELAND

CHARLES MURPHY

CRESCENT BOOKS
NEW YORK

To my mother and father.

Text
Charles Murphy

Design
Jill Coote

Research
Carrie Fonseca
Leora Kahn

Editorial
David Gibbon
Aindreas McEntee
Fergal Tobin

Commissioning
Andrew Preston
Laura Potts
Miriam Sharland

Production
Ruth Arthur
David Proffit
Sally Connolly
Andrew Whitelaw

Director of Production
Gerald Hughes

The publishers would like to acknowledge the particular assistance of Carrie Fonseca and The Slide File without whom this book would not have been possible.

Right: *Kilkenny Castle, County Kilkenny.*
Previous pages: *Clew Bay, County Mayo.*
First page: *round tower and church, Swords, County Dublin.*

CONTENTS

INTRODUCTION

"Maybe ... it's nearly time we had a little less respect for the dead, an' a little more regard for the livin'." Thus spoke one of Sean O'Casey's characters in his play, *Juno and the Paycock*, and they are perhaps appropriate words with which to begin a consideration of the history of Ireland. Has Ireland's past not been overstressed, its dead cherished rather too much? Would not a healthy "regard for the livin'." involve the forgetting of much of Ireland's complicated and often painful past?

Yet the relation between the dead and the living, between past and present in Ireland is far too important for such arguments to carry any real conviction. It is only through an appreciation of its rich and varied past that Ireland's rich and varied present can be understood. The purpose of this book is to present Irish history accurately but accessibly through words and pictures. The text follows the story from Ireland's first inhabitants right through to the twentieth century, and it is complemented by hundreds of pictures which reflect the enormous range of Irish experience through the centuries.

The text looks first at Ireland pre-1169, dealing with early human settlement, the arrival of the Celts, the coming of Christianity, the importance of kingship and the role of the Vikings. It then considers the period 1169-1603, covering the Anglo-Norman invasion and the complex web of political relationships which subsequently developed. The next section deals with 1603-1800, plantation, rebellion, suppression, and parliamentarianism all forming part of the story. The years 1800-1920 involve the struggles for Catholic emancipation and for repeal of the union with Britain, the tragedy of the mid-nineteenth century famine, the emergence of the Home Rule movement, the importance of the politics of land, and the development of the forces of early twentieth century nationalism and unionism. Lastly, the text looks at Ireland since 1920, at the painful birth of a partitioned island and the growth of the two Irish states.

Alongside the study of persistent themes within Irish history, there also appears in these pages a colourful catalogue of individuals who have played significant roles in Ireland's unfolding story: St Patrick, Colum Cille, Brian Ború, Strongbow, Gerald of Wales, Hugh O'Neill, Oliver Cromwell, James II, William III, Jonathan Swift, Henry Grattan, Theobald Wolfe Tone, Daniel O'Connell, Thomas Davis, Charles Stewart Parnell, Oscar Wilde, Patrick Pearse, Arthur Griffith, Eamon de Valera, Michael Collins, Edward Carson, James Craig, William Cosgrave, Terence O'Neill, Ian Paisley, Charles Haughey, Mary Robinson.

Some of these names are capable of arousing not only fascination but also strong emotional response. That, in a sense, is the excitement and the curse of Irish history. Thus Patrick Pearse, for example, is both historical man and hero, as compelling for the historian as he is loved or hated by many for his role as a republican martyr. This book attempts to reflect the richness of Irish history, but to do so with appropriate historical balance. It tries – through words and images – to present the often complex and passionate events which make up Ireland's past in such a way that their true colour remains. But it also seeks to set these events in a historical context which will render them meaningful, and which will help to avoid the pointless simplicities still favoured by some. To show true "respect for the dead" involves portraying their lives and their world as fully and accurately as possible, and this can only enhance the lives of those who are still "livin'."

Above: *the Proleek Dolmen, Ballymascanlan, County Louth.*

Below: the Bank of Ireland, College Green, Dublin.

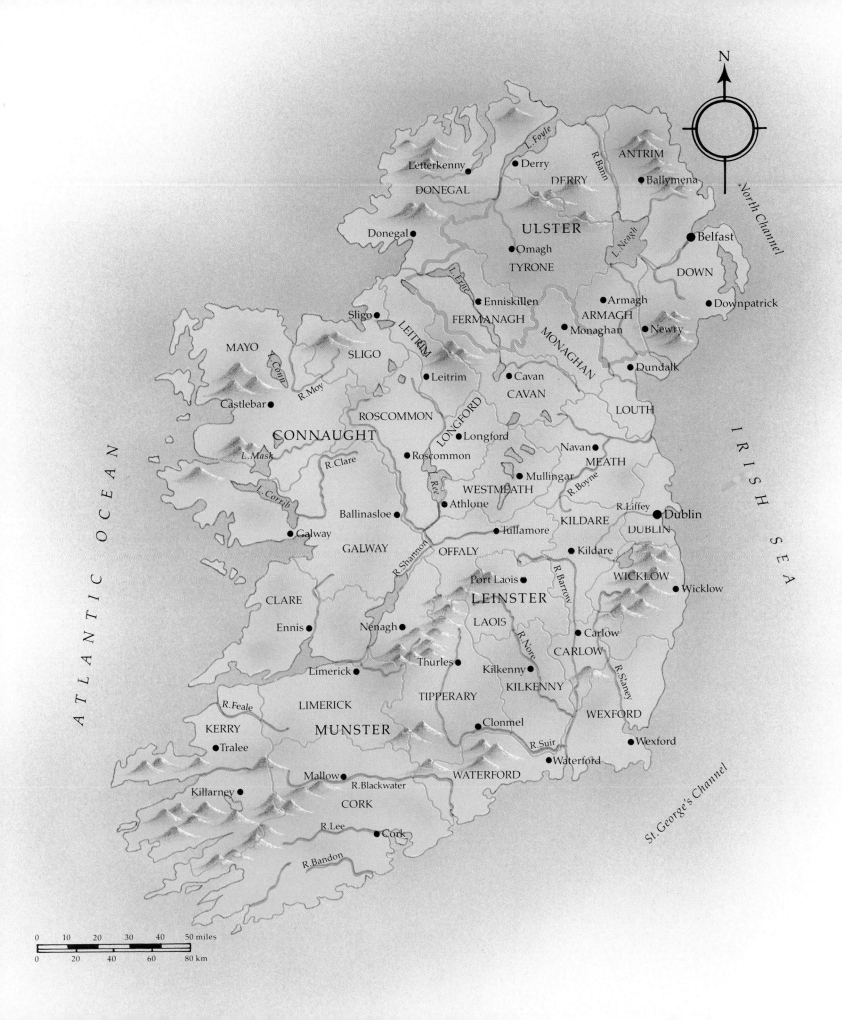

CHAPTER ONE
ORIGINS

IRELAND PRE-1169

*The truth is rarely pure
and never simple.*

OSCAR WILDE

Writing in the first century A.D., the Roman historian, Tacitus, claimed that Ireland lay 'between Britain and Spain'. No such confusion persists today. Yet much does remain unclear about Ireland's history, and the awkward task facing the Irish historian is that of clarifying while avoiding simplification.

The first traces of human settlement in Ireland date from 7000 B.C. These people appear to have lived by means of hunting and fishing. By 4,000 B.C., the inhabitants of New Stone Age Ireland had developed a more advanced approach to subsistence with their ability to cultivate land. These Neolithic farmers also built a variety of megalithic (large stone) tombs – further evidence of a certain sophistication. Around the year A.D. 200 Ireland's Bronze Age metalworkers were making use of domestic deposits as well as engaging in trade beyond the island. Irish daggers and axes found their way to Europe, while some of the tin used in Ireland appears to have originated in Spain. The fact that Ireland lay on the periphery of

Europe did not mean it was necessarily aloof in terms of culture or economy. As one authority, Michael Richter, has observed:

Ireland was remote only in the geographical sense. Both in antiquity and in the Middle Ages, the sea proved more of a link with the outside world than a barrier.

Evidence from such periods is sketchy, but the Late Bronze Age in Ireland produced many artefacts which tempted and taunted historians. Its distinctive bronze swords and shields suggest a pride in truly martial arts, and Dublin's National Museum possesses a fine collection of such pieces.

Early Ireland is associated in many people's minds with the Celts. Yet on their arrival during the latter part of the first millennium B.C. their character was that of immigrant bullies. They came as a powerful minority, influenced by the indigenous population which they encountered and dominated. Iron-using farmers, the Celts shifted east, south and west from

Previous pages:
Poulnabrone dolmen, County Clare, the imposing remains of a chambered tomb.

Facing page: *a stone circle at Loughcrew, County Meath. Some Irish stone circles, many of which date from the Bronze Age, appear to have been built as observatories.*

Below: *a dolmen at Ardara, County Donegal, in the northwest of Ireland. The heavy capstone is supported by standing stones.*

central Europe and arrived in Ireland by a variety of routes. They came to dominate the island, and while traces of pre-Celtic languages can be found it was Irish-Gaelic which came to prevail. The Irish-Gaelic language represented a distinctive, locally influenced version of Celtic. Early Irish literature contains evidence of certain continental traits – including head-hunting – but this should not lead one into the automatic assumption that all in Ireland was continentally Celtic. Tara (County Meath) held a symbolically crucial place in the kingship world of the Celts in Ireland. But it was a cultural focal point long before the Celts arrived on the island. Continuity as well as change helped mould the life of the Irish Celts.

It has often been commented upon that Ireland did not experience Roman invasion. In his life of Agricola (a Roman governor of Britain during the first century A.D.), Tacitus tells us that, 'The whole side of Britain that faces Ireland was lined with [Agricola's] forces'. The historian further asserts that he

> *often heard Agricola say that Ireland could be reduced and held by a single legion and a few auxiliaries, and that the conquest would also pay from the point of view of Britain, if Roman arms were in evidence on every side and liberty vanished off the map.*

But while no attempt was made by the Romans to conquer Ireland, there was a Roman influence. Archaeological evidence points to contact with Roman culture prior to the departure from Britain (in A.D. 409) of the last Roman legions. There appears, for example, to have been a notable trade in wine, and some Roman objects date from as early as the first century A.D. Remains in Ireland demonstrate that during the fifth century A.D. there was considerable contact with Roman culture.

Indeed, the inhabitants of Ireland on occasions harassed those of the neighbouring island. From the third century A.D. onwards Roman Britain experienced significant attacks from a variety of marauders, among them the Saxons and the Irish. In A.D. 367 a threefold threat materialised from the north (Picts), the east (Saxons) and the west (Irish). With the effective demise of Roman authority early in the fifth century A.D. raids appear to have resulted in settlements and more lasting conquests. The Irish established themselves most significantly in what

are now Scotland and Wales. In Scotland the language of the Picts was soon replaced by that of the incoming Irish, so effective was the incursion. Indeed, the name of the region derives from the title of the Irish (or *Scoti*) who established themselves there. It was from the northeast of Ireland – the kingdom of the Dal Riada – that the Irish who settled in Argyll originated. Exactly when and why they did set out for the neighbouring land is not clear. Whatever their motivation the Argyll base facilitated further settlements, though naturally the development of Irish influence in the new land was one of gradual progress. There is at least one literary reference to a Pictish king still ruling over Argyll during the latter part of the sixth century A.D. But the Irish conquest in Scotland was certainly impressive – if invasion and settlement can ever be deemed so. This was the most successful process of Irish colonisation in Britain, and the Dal Riada dynasty came eventually to control the land of the Picts with Cinaed mac Ailpin (Kenneth mac Alpine) ruling between 843 and 858.

There was also important Irish settlement in Wales. To the north (Anglesea, Carnarvonshire and Denbighshire) colonists from Leinster ruled for a time. They left their mark on Gwynedd in the name of the Lleyn peninsula, derived from Leinster's Laigin dynasty. During the fifth century A.D. these Irish rulers were driven out by Cunedda (a British king) but there was more significant Irish settlement in South

Left: *Newgrange, County Meath, site of one of the world's most impressive Neolithic tombs, built in the fourth century B.C.*

Right: *sunshine penetrates the Newgrange tomb.*

Wales (Cardiganshire, Carmarthenshire and Pembrokeshire). Coming from what is now Cork, Kerry and Waterford, the Irish rulers belonged to the Deisi dynasty and brought with them their Irish language. The famous *Ogham* inscriptions provide valuable evidence of such settlement patterns. *Ogham* script was a simple style of lettering which used lines and notches carved along the vertical edge of a stone. The alphabet employed is based on the Latin, and these stones therefore reflect the meeting of Irish and Roman cultures. Employed on the memorials of leading figures, *Ogham* is the earliest written Irish, and although the inscriptions are mostly very simple they none the less provide valuable evidence of early Irish culture. *Ogham* stone memorials have been found in Wales and throughout Ireland (particularly to the south). They date from a lengthy period (fifth to seventh centuries A.D.) and provide tangible proof of the extent of Irish settlement in Britain. Not only did Irish culture persist in parts of the larger island, but at least some of the Irish plainly maintained their

Above: *a wooden finial. Ornaments such as this were often placed on the top of a roof or on the corners of a tower.*

Below: *a bronze urn, produced in approximately 700 B.C. and found near Castlederg in County Tyrone, Northern Ireland.*

Left: *a bronze sword hilt. Dublin's National Museum contains a fine collection of Bronze Age and Iron Age metalwork.*

Right: *a bronze sword. Such items represent clear evidence of a martial culture in Ireland.*

language while in Britain. Inscriptions written in Irish indicate that this language was familiar to those of the more elevated classes whose status merited *Ogham* memorial stones.

The interaction of cultures was having its effect in Ireland too. It appears that Romano-British culture reached the smaller island, and it is also possible that the process of Irish raiding in Britain affected power relations back in Ireland. The Laigin, as we have seen, made significant inroads into Wales and evidence exists within Laigin literary culture of words borrowed from the Latin. Invasion appears to have led to a process of cultural exchange. This, again, was to prove a resilient – though complicated – feature of Irish experience in relation to Britain.

Indeed, Irish Christianity itself owed much to British influence, and the most celebrated figure in Ireland's Christian history – Patrick – was himself born in Britain. The case of Ireland's patron saint in some ways reflects much that has been important in Irish experience. Patrick is, perhaps, an appropriate

figure for Ireland to celebrate. The dates of his birth and death are not known, though it is generally accepted that he was active as a missionary in Ireland during the fifth century A.D. Much is still vague, but he was the son of a Roman official and was born in the west of Britain. During his teens he was captured by Irish raiders and taken to Ireland, where he worked as a shepherd and where he stayed for approximately six years. During this period he became a devoted Christian, though it was by means of a pagan crew that he managed to effect his escape from Ireland, having first travelled two hundred miles to reach the coast. The ship was bound for the European mainland, but Patrick eventually returned to Britain. There, thoughts of Ireland lived with him and he returned to the island of his captivity – this time with the intention of preaching the Christian gospel.

Patrick is often given credit for the conversion of the pagan Irish and the establishment of the church in Ireland. But the shift to Christianity was much

Below: *detail from a bronze shield, found in County Limerick. The shield dates from the eighth century B.C.*

more complicated than this and deserves some attention, particularly in the light of the religion's subsequent importance through centuries of Irish life. The chronicler, Prosper of Aquitaine, records for the year A.D. 431 that Pope Celestine sent Palladius 'as the first bishop to the Irish who believe in Christ'. The traditional date given for Patrick's missionary landing in Ireland is A.D. 432. In fact the 432 tradition is unreliable, but there is other evidence which suggests the borrowing of Latin Christian terms into the Irish language during the first half of the fourth century A.D.. Thus it may be assumed that a sturdy Christian community existed in Patrick's chosen island during the century *preceding* his missionary activity there. The cult of Patrick had become widely popular in Ireland by the late seventh century, and indeed it continues to enjoy widespread adherence (at least once a year) even in modern times. But it would be simplistic to attribute to Patrick the winning of the Irish to the faith. It is simply not known when the first Christian missionaries started to proselytise in Ireland. It is possible that the solidly structured church of Gaul provided the godly troops for the religious invasion during the fourth century.

Some scholars have suggested that our understanding of Patrick in fact represents the bringing together of accounts relating to two separate figures, the confusion arising because Patricius was the second name of the aforementioned bishop, Palladius. Certainly it could be argued that there has been an over-concentration by historians on the words and actions of Patrick, to the detriment of a wider and fuller grasp of events surrounding fourth and fifth century Christianity in Ireland; other missionaries have perhaps been short-changed in accounts of this period. Yet, whatever the merits of figures such as Auxilius or Iserninus, it is to Patrick that we are forced repeatedly to turn. Muirchu's *Vita Patricii (Life of Patrick)* – written towards the end of

Above: *a reconstruction in County Clare of a crannog, or lake dwelling. Crannogs provided safe dwelling places in times of danger.*

Right: *Staigue ring fort in County Kerry, the drystone walls of which are four metres thick.*

Facing page: *beehive huts, Skellig Michael, off the coast of Kerry in the southwest of Ireland. The huts form part of a monastery that was plundered by Vikings in the ninth century.*

the seventh century – asserts that Iserninus and Auxilius were made bishops in Gaul along with Patrick, but mentions them no further. Patrick, however, is portrayed as the medium controlling the elements and even bringing the dead back to life. Even if healthy scepticism is applied to such accounts, Patrick remains an important figure for the study of this period in Ireland's past. The two surviving texts attributed to him (the *Confession* and the *Letter to the soldiers of Coroticus*) are different in purpose. The first includes a justification of his work in Ireland and a personal confession of faith by the author. The *Letter*, on the other hand, was written with a view to securing the liberation of some of Patrick's recent Irish converts to Christianity, who had been sold to the Picts as slaves. These two works are important items but they leave many questions unanswered. The *Confession*, for example, contains no specific dates, and neither of the works was meant by its author to offer a detailed, historical account of Ireland's conversion to Christianity. It does appear that Patrick boldly went where no Christian missionary had gone before, but he is unfortunately rather vague about these newly penetrated areas.

What is certain is that Ireland did in time become a Christian island. While pre-Christian, Irish Celtic tradition was preserved (at least in literary form) in the twelfth century *Book of Invasions*, it was Christianity which was to define much of the developing Irish culture. Patrick seems to have encouraged people towards monasticism, and with the spread of Christianity in Ireland monasteries provided valuable centres for the corporate expression of the new religion. Great monasteries such as those of Clonard, Cork or Kildare were powerful ecclesiastical communities. They enjoyed enviable wealth and influence, and were well connected with the powerful in society. Early in the ninth century, for example, the king of Leinster lived at Kildare as did his brother (who was abbot) and his sister (who was abbess).

As with many other areas of Irish life, significant individuals appear to have become important cult figures and to have left tangible monuments to their particular vision. St Finnian, for instance, founded the monastery at Clonard (County Meath) in the sixth century. He was also reputed to have been the inspiration for other monastic founders such as St Ciaran, who established a monastery at Clonmacnois (County Offaly). In addition, Ciaran appears to have been influenced by St Enda of Aran who was – in turn – reputedly taught by the fifth century British saint, Ninian. Thus a web of monastic cult and foundation influenced the Irish church. For even if the supposed guru-apostle relationships mentioned above did not in reality exist, it would still be instructive that such traditions were *created*

Above: *an* Ogham *stone, Dunloe, County Kerry.* Ogham *inscriptions involved lines and notches carved along the vertical edge of a stone.*

Facing page: *a standing stone at Eyeries in County Cork which, at over five metres high, is one of the tallest in Ireland.*

Right: *a standing stone at Clogher Head, County Kerry. Some stones were used for marking graves.*

Overleaf: *the monastery at Clonmacnoise. Founded by St Ciaran in the sixth century, this was ransacked by the English in the sixteenth century.*

surrounding these major monastic figures. St Colum Cille – for whom, again, Finnian was reputedly a source of inspiration – is important not only because of his contemporary influence, but also because of Adomnan's Life; this account of Colum Cille – written c.700 by an abbot of Iona – offers us helpful insights into the life of the period. Colum Cille (or Columba the Elder) was born in 521-522. Having established the monastic communities at Derry and Durrow he moved (in 563) to Iona, an island off the west Scottish coast. It was here that he came to base his work and it was here that he died, in 597. The membership of the initial community at Iona included monks of Irish, British and Germanic extraction. The monastic existence on Iona was rather isolated and austere. Geography and climate saw to that! But there is considerable divergence of opinion regarding the severity of discipline called for by Colum Cille.

Accounts such as that by Adomnan must be treated cautiously. After all, it was written about a century after Colum Cille's death and is far too reverential. But it does touch on important themes regarding the society and culture of the contemporary Ireland. Adomnan records, for example, that Colum Cille ordained a king of the Ui Neill dynasty (Aedan) on Iona. Too much should not be read into such accounts. But the relation of the church to the wider

society is indeed vital. During the seventh and eighth centuries there emerged legal writings which have greatly enhanced our perception of the ecclesiastical and of the wider culture at this time in Ireland. Scholars in Ireland had maintained and cultivated Irish; to this Latin was added. It seems that rigorous study of this additional language began in Ireland in the latter part of the sixth century. During the following two centuries law tracts started to be written down. *Senchas Mar* (a collection of tracts apparently compiled in the early eighth century) and the *Collectio Canonum Hibernensis* (originating from the same period) provide much legally focused information about Irish society and in particular about church culture. For it was within the church's orbit that scholarly sophistication developed. In Latin and in Irish, for secular as for religious society, ecclesiastical scholarship provided the foundation for seventh and eighth century law.

The Old Testament was important in this process: in the *Collectio Canonum Hibernensis* considerable time is taken up with quotations from this source as well as from significant church fathers. The *Collectio* in fact also deals with widespread social issues, including those of theft and inheritance. Sanctuary, too, was dealt with in this text. The area around a sacred site was held to ensure protection for laity as it did for clerics. At the end of the seventh century 'Adomnan's Law' (the Law of the Innocent) had placed not only the clergy but also women and children under protection for the duration of war. Thus ecclesiastical law-makers greatly influenced the world beyond as well as that within the church.

The writings of clerics at this time also reflect the development of the idea of the divinely ordained monarch. So in medieval Ireland the Almighty came to play a significant role in the theory of monarchy. This was a naturally complementary relationship. Competing kings could only gain through religious sanction – who better to have on your side than God? For their part, clerics belonged to a religious culture which enjoyed much wealth and status; solid, favourable royal authority offered a welcome basis for stability. A passage drawn from a treatise written in the seventh century reflects this emphasis upon the blessings of good kingship:

> *The justness of the king is the peace of the peoples, the protection of the land, the invulnerability and protection of the people, care for the weak, the joy of the people, mildness of the air and calmness of the sea, fertility of the soil, consolation for the poor, the heritage of the sons, the hope for future salvation, the abundance of corn and the fruitfulness of the trees.*

An impressive catalogue indeed!

Despite their ideological reliance upon ecclesiastics, medieval Irish kings were a truly powerful force. In fact, ideas of royal rule seem not to have drawn solely from the Christian well. The *Audacht Morainn (Bequest of Morann)* displays very few debts to Christian thinking. Written around the year 700 and emerging from southern Ireland, the *Bequest* presents the ruler as the embodiment of his people, with appropriate responsibility: his good behaviour results in great benefit for those over whom he presides. The problem with such priceless sources is that persistent attempts to inculcate good behaviour suggest, if anything, a gap between noble ideal and contemporary action. Strong oral tradition can be traced in the *Bequest*, for example; more than one generation plainly felt it necessary that the advice which this treatise contained regarding healthy kingship should be expressed.

Much remains unclear about Irish kingship in the middle ages. There seem to have been layers of monarchy, from the person presiding over a local kingdom (the *ri tuaithe*), through the ruler who was Lord over a number of local kings (the *ruiri*), to the provincial king (the *ri ruirech*) who actually exercised considerable influence, certainly by the eighth century. The annals (chronicles, the first of which

Left: *the High Cross of Moone in County Kildare. This dates from the ninth century and is decorated with human and animal forms.*

Right: *a roadside statue of St Colum Cille. This sixth-century saint established monastic communities in Derry, Durrow and on Iona.*

Far right: *a round tower and St Kevin's Church, Glendalough, County Wicklow. The tower is thirty-one metres high.*

Below: *the Gallarus Oratory on the Dingle Peninsula, County Kerry, a fine stone oratory dating from the eighth century.*

Left: *a portrait of St John in the eighth-century* Book of Kells. *This beautiful illuminated manuscript can be seen in Trinity College, Dublin.*

Below: *a standing stone in Glencolumbkille in County Donegal.*

appears to have been begun on Iona in the latter part of the sixth century) reflect the dominance of this provincial class of monarch and, again, the intermingling of church authority and secular rule can be detected. In the south of Ireland Artri mac Cathail was ordained at the end of the eighth century as king of Munster; he in turn permitted the church which had ordained him to demand tax from the province over which his rule had been religiously sanctioned.

The notion of a high king (or *ard-ri*) is an important one and has generated much debate and speculation. It has been suggested that Niall of the Nine Hostages (Niall Noigiallach, from whom the Ui Neill dynasty took its name, and who died around the middle of the fifth century) might have been the first Irish ruler to adopt the title of high king. If this is true, then it was a royal claim lacking substance. *Effective* rule over the whole island eluded even later Irish kings, though it was closest to being brought to life at the very point at which twelfth century invasion rendered it impossible. Despite the power of certain rulers – particularly those of the Ui Neill – it is too convenient (and unhistorical) to assume a high king model for Ireland in this period. Claims of authority over the whole island contrast with a fierce reality of local dynastic power and competition.

Less lofty heights existed, of course, than those inhabited by kings. The ruler presided over his people (or *tuath*). The royal *derbfine* (the close family clan) enjoyed the right of succession. The early eighth century law tract *Crith Gablach* uses the word *tanaise* to denote the individual due to succeed the existing ruler. The identity of this person appears to have been agreed upon during the lifetime of the king from whom they were due to inherit. Below kings lay lords (or *flaithi*). Members of this class had clients – the more the better, in terms of one's social status! Those bound to a nobleman in this way consisted of freemen, and the relationship was a contractual one. The lord offered protection and the loan of cattle for grazing his client's land; in return the freeman provided rent. The freeman class contained gradations of status, but they were all of higher standing than the serfs (or *senchleithe*). This class was divided by legal writers into different categories and its members were bound to their noble's estate. The complicated picture was compounded by the prevalence in the period of polygamy, divorce and remarriage.

Just as in pre-Christian Ireland druids had fulfilled the role of a learned as well as a priestly class, so after the coming of Christianity scholarly, intellectual functions were performed by ecclesiastical figures. Although most clerical scholars in the early Christian period had noble backgrounds, they are perhaps better seen as a distinct class; certainly their contribution was a distinctive one. Irish illuminated manuscripts are justly famous. The most celebrated are the *Book of Durrow* (seventh century) and the *Book of Kells* (eighth century) – both held now by Trinity College, Dublin. Sculpture and metalwork also survive and, again, the role of the church was vital here. Indeed, there are discernible similarities between these various art forms. The motifs on certain sculpted crosses resemble those in illuminated texts such as

Right: *the eighth-century Ardagh Chalice. Made of bronze and silver, this was found in County Limerick.*

Right: *a gold earring. Some Irish gold ornaments were exported to Europe even before the arrival in Ireland of the Celts.*

Facing page: *the hill of Tara, County Meath. Tara was an important symbolic site in the history of Irish kingship.*

the *Book of Durrow*. Metalwork had had a long pedigree in Ireland even by the seventh century. Pre-Christian workers had been familiar with the processes involved in enamelling for many centuries, and we are fortunate in the survival of medieval Irish pieces such as bells and brooches. The famous Tara Brooch and Ardagh

Left: *the Tara Brooch, dating from the early eighth century and a classic example of Irish metalwork expertise.*

Chalice are classic examples of Irish metalworking expertise.

Large numbers of Irish artefacts were taken to Scandinavia by a group of actors whose role in medieval Irish history was both important at the time and famous well after it – the Vikings. Attitudes towards the Viking impact on Ireland (as elsewhere in Europe) have varied greatly. The image of the rampaging hooligan has come to be complemented by that of the more constructive contributor to Irish society and culture. Neither stereotype will do; the important thing is that both must be examined. Violence had been known in pre-Viking Ireland, but the late-eighth-century attacks by Scandinavians represented the beginning of an important phase in the island's historical development. In 795 the east coast island of Lambay was raided. Colum Cille had founded a monastery on this island, and another site of his monastic work – Iona – was also attacked in 795. Iona, indeed, was to suffer again at Viking hands, and after the killing of monks there in 806 the surviving members of the community moved to mainland Ireland, setting up a monastery in Kells, County Meath, which they completed in 814. Although the Viking raids were geographically concentrated, they nonetheless represented a significant tide of onslaught. Monasteries were ill-equipped to fend off marauders, and Viking mobility gave them a fearsome advantage in these early raiding years. Oblivious to rules regarding sacred Christian

*Little Skellig, County Kerry,
in the southwest of Ireland.*

sites, the Scandinavian intruders were greeted with understandable horror on the part of the clerical community and this response is (not surprisingly) evident in monastic chronicles of the period.

By 823 the whole of the Irish coast had been negotiated by the unwelcome tourists, and although Irish retaliation was not unknown the trend was with the Vikings (most of whom came to Ireland from Norway). During the early decades the attacks had a random quality, but Viking involvement was to change in character after the first third of the ninth century. Attacks intensified and in the 830s there occurred the first known inland raid of any significance. As with the first wave, Irish experience reflected a broader pattern. In 793 – just two years before Lambay and Iona were hit – Lindisfarne monastery, off the northeast coast of England, had been attacked. So in the 830s raids in England as in Ireland became more concentrated. In 837 major Viking fleets cruised the rivers Boyne and Liffey. Three years later Scandinavians wintered in Ireland, a telling indication of the settlement which was to follow.

Monks wrote about many horrific experiences at the hands of the Vikings. But the historical record for a long time underplayed those aspects of the Norsemen's contribution which were positive. Many important Irish towns (among them Dublin, Cork, Limerick, Waterford and Wexford) have their origins in Scandinavian settlement. Naturally enough, once the Vikings took root they 'went native' and became involved in the locally based dynastic conflicts which Ireland had known prior to their arrival. As early as the 840s, indeed, there is evidence of collusion between Norse and Irish, and this was soon to become a frequent phenomenon. Dublin was the first Viking settlement and was destined to become the most significant one. The year 841 marks its foundation.

Ten years later tussles began between different groups of Scandinavians. The arrival of Danes in 851 appears to have irritated Norwegian Dublin, though the newcomers eventually established a place for themselves there. In considering such developments the links with England should not be forgotten. It was via England that the Danes had come to Ireland, and they seem subsequently to have kept up contact with Scandinavian settlers there. The interests of the Viking newcomers to Ireland altered as their approach shifted from that of raiding to that of establishing a more lasting base on the island. They began to direct their energies towards longer term economic strategies. Irish ports grew in relative importance,

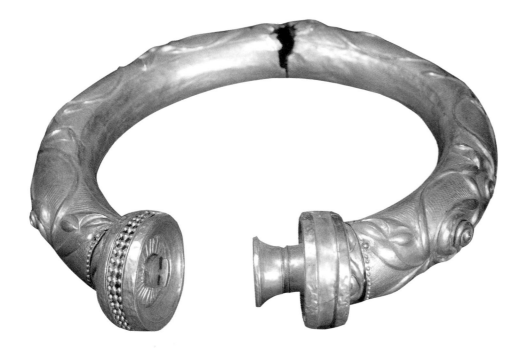

focal points for the development of trade. Any general impact which the Viking immigrants did have on kingship would probably have occurred anyway. The existing small kingdoms began to disappear in this period, with the *ri tuaithe* gradually diminishing in importance. But this shift appears to have begun prior to the arrival of the Vikings.

During the ninth century three dynasties had come to dominant prominence: the Ui Neill, the Eoganachta and the Dal Cais. Cashel (where the Eoganachta were based) fell in 964 to the Dal Cais, and with the succession to the Dal Cais monarchy of Brian Boru in 976 there arrived on the dynastic scene one of Ireland's most famed heroic figures. Born around the year 940, Brian came to achieve notable success against allied Norse and Irish, and by the 980s controlled the southern part of Ireland. His aim was to become effective high king of the island, and by 1002 Mael Sechnaill II (king of the rival Ui Neill) had yielded to him. Between then and 1014 Brian enjoyed wide authority. In 1006 he even travelled unchallenged around the north of Ireland – far from

Above: *a gold bracelet from Gleninsheen, County Clare, dating from the seventh century B.C.*

Right: *a gold lunula found at Broighter in County Derry, Northern Ireland.*

and Dublin witnessed its first minting of a silver coinage. Killers and traders, destroyers and builders, bullies and innovators – their role was a complicated one. Violence did not, of course, disappear with settlement. While the Ui Neill swept the northern coast free of Scandinavian strongholds during the latter ninth century, it should also be noted that sporadic Viking attacks on northern Irish sites continued, Armagh suffering on more than one occasion during this period.

The newcomers certainly altered the details of Irish Kingship as a result of particular campaigns and conflicts. Following the start of the second Viking wave early in the tenth century, there occurred in 919 a battle in Dublin which resulted in victory for the Scandinavians over Niall Glundub (king of the Ui Neill) who was himself killed. But is it possible, from such instances, to discern some wider pattern of Viking influence over the important structure of the Irish kingdom? Comparison with English experience provides a useful perspective. There the Vikings took control of entire kingdoms; in the eleventh century, indeed, the Danes gained influence over the national kingship. This was not the case in Ireland, where Scandinavian kingdoms were comparatively small and where innovation lay in the fact that the new towns often provided useful

Right: *a Viking coin from the tenth century. Coins are a valuable source of information for historians.*

Below: *the Battle of Clontarf, 1014, in which Brian Boru defeated an alliance of Leinstermen and Vikings.*

his Munster base. During these comparatively peaceful years he contributed, among other things, to the restoration of churches and libraries in Ireland. But in 1014 he was killed at the battle of Clontarf (situated now on the north side of Dublin). In this contest Brian did not have as his objective the freeing of Ireland from Viking authority; he had in fact shown himself perfectly prepared to ally with Waterford Vikings. While Clontarf was indeed fought against an alliance of Vikings and Leinstermen, it should be understood for what it actually was: part of the familiar pattern of dynastic conflict within Ireland.

Although the battle was won, the death of Brian halted him precisely when he seemed to be on the point of giving some real substance to the idea of a kingship of Ireland. Battles between chieftains for overall control were also evident in the following century. The tussles between twelfth century kings were complex and protracted, and it was as a result of such a conflict that one of Ireland's most famous events emerged: the invasion of 1169.

CHAPTER TWO
CONQUESTS
1169 – 1603

*But although they are fully endowed with
natural gifts, their external characteristics of
beard and dress, and internal cultivation of the
mind, are so barbarous that they cannot be said
to have any culture ... They are a wild and
inhospitable people.*
GERALD OF WALES

The year 1169 was indeed an important point in Ireland's history. It introduced the island to a new and more lasting phase of incomplete conquest. The reasons behind the Anglo-Norman invasion are at once complex and simple. The Norman assault on England had taken place in 1066. During the twelfth century significant economic links existed between Ireland and Britain; trade involving Dublin and parts of the west of Britain appears to have flourished in the early twelfth century during the reign of Henry I in England. But if Ireland was part of a wider economic unit, the prize of effective Irish kingship remained a cherished (though elusive) one. Efforts towards cohesion were, as ever, complemented by the tensions. This should not lead one into any casual dismissal of the idea of an Irish nation in this period. Nationhood was rather undeveloped at this time. Nor, however, can one happily swallow the idea of a united nation, harmonious and undivided.

Into this picture of ambiguous nationhood were drawn external forces, from England. In the early twelfth century Turloch O'Connor of Connacht pressed a claim to the kingship of Ireland, and his son (Rory O'Connor) continued the trend later in the century. Rory's ally, Tiernan O'Rourke (king of Breifne), celebrated O'Connor's assumption of the high kingship in 1166 by attempting to gain revenge over Dermot MacMurrough (king of Leinster). MacMurrough had abducted O'Rourke's wife (Dervorgilla) in 1152 and, although she had in fact returned to O'Rourke, the latter appears to have retained considerable feelings of hostility towards the Leinster ruler. The rivalry between the two men did not derive solely from the conflict over Dervorgilla, but their mutual antipathy was given extra bite by this episode. With his ally as high king, O'Rourke was in a position to punish his rival and MacMurrough was driven out of Leinster. The dethroned Dermot turned to Henry II (king of England, 1154-89), to whom he gave his allegiance. In return Henry granted MacMurrough permission to seek aid from among his subjects. The idea of invading Ireland was not entirely alien to Henry's thinking; it had, in fact, been considered shortly after his accession. Indeed, Pope Adrian IV had blessed Henry and his heirs with the right to rule Ireland – an irony, given the religious contours which Anglo-Irish relations were later to follow.

It was not, however, Henry II who invaded Ireland in the first instance; his own inheritance in England had been shaky enough at the start of his reign and he decided against personal intervention in Ireland at first. Certain of his nobles did, however, take up the challenge. The Anglo-Norman, Strongbow (Richard FitzGilbert de Clare, earl of Pembroke), accepted an exchange which was to have huge historical side effects. Strongbow was to receive in marriage Aoife, MacMurrough's daughter, and was also promised the Leinster succession upon Dermot's demise. In return Strongbow pledged to help put MacMurrough back on the Leinster throne. It was actually in 1167 that Dermot travelled back to Ireland (accompanied by a small, mixed force of Welsh, Normans and Flemings) but the more famous date of 1169 marked the arrival of the first significant Norman contingent in Ireland. Landing in county Wexford, they were met by a force of local Vikings but these quickly gave way to the invaders. In 1170 Strongbow himself arrived, captured Waterford and married Aoife. Dublin soon fell to the incoming soldiers, and when Dermot MacMurrough died in 1171 Strongbow became king of Leinster. Predictably, Rory O'Connor fought on, laying siege to the Normans in Dublin. But Strongbow's military superiority made possible their successful defence of Dublin in 1171. The newcomers were not going to be dislodged.

This point was not lost on Henry II, who decided to set himself up as overlord of Ireland and who consequently landed at Waterford in October 1171, backed by a formidable army. It is possible that the thinking behind this move was not quite as simple as it might initially seem. Certainly Henry did not want to allow the emergence of an independent Irish kingdom under rival rule, and was therefore keen to emphasise his own authority over Strongbow. This he quickly achieved, with Richard offering his submission to Henry's supremacy and being allowed to hold Leinster as a fief. The English ruler retained Dublin, and his power was further underlined by the submission of the kings in southeast Ireland. Large tracts, to the west and to the north, were still beyond his grasp, but his intrusion into Ireland had none the less proved effective. Even the Irish clergy pledged him their allegiance.

But the tugging of Strongbow's lead was not necessarily the only thought in Henry's mind when he directed his attentions toward Ireland. Ireland provided a possible lordship which Henry could bestow on his young son, John. Furthermore, he might have wished to capitalise on the papal endorsement which he had received regarding Ireland. The famous Bull, *Laudabiliter*, by which Adrian IV had given Henry permission to rule Ireland, might have been interpreted as lending a certain legitimacy to the king's own desires. Such a claim must undoubtedly be judged to have been spurious. But its usefulness would not have been lost on the English king, particularly in the light of the recent killing of archbishop Thomas a Becket in December 1170. The murder had caused strained relations between the king and the church, but Henry's keenness to portray himself as a church reformer

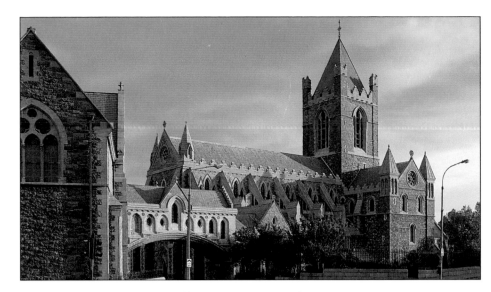

demonstrates his awareness of the value of a favourable relationship with the ecclesiastical community. In 1172 he made his peace with the church and was actually endorsed in his authority by Pope Alexander III.

In fact, the Irish church had been significantly reformed without help or influence from England. St Malachy was the most influential of the reformers of this period, apparently born at the end of the eleventh century and becoming archbishop of Armagh in 1132. Five years later he retired to Bangor. But he was later sent to Rome to procure proof of papal endorsement for the archbishops of Cashel and of Armagh. This trip was to emerge as an important one. For on his way to Rome Malachy encountered and was impressed by St Bernard, leading French ecclesiastic and founder of the abbey

KING HENRY THE II.nd

Left: *King Henry II of England, who played a key role in the twelfth-century Anglo-Norman invasion of Ireland.*

Right: *St Patrick's Cathedral, Dublin. One of the city's oldest places of worship, this became a cathedral in 1192.*

at Clairvaux. Malachy later sent people to be trained at Clairvaux (where Bernard was the head of the Cistercian order) and in 1142 Ireland's first Cistercian foundation was established at Mellifont (county Louth). Further foundations followed and the Cistercians subsequently became an influential order within Ireland.

The synod of Kells in 1152 (four years after Malachy's death) restructured the Irish church, with Armagh, Cashel, Dublin and Tuam all being recognised as archbishoprics and thirty-six dioceses being established throughout the island. The archbishop of Armagh was declared to be the Primate of All Ireland, and so the northward shift in influence which Malachy had helped bring about thus became institutionalised in Irish ecclesiastical structure. Lasting, too, were the architectural results of twelfth-century church reform. New dioceses received new cathedrals, many of which survive in ruined form to this day. So prior to Henry II's intervention the Irish church had been shuffling itself into a different order, reorganising and restructuring and reforming on a significant scale.

What of the wider society and culture of twelfth century Ireland? One of the most important sources for this period is the record of Gerald of Wales. Giraldus de Barri – referred to as Giraldus Cambrensis owing to his having originated in Cambria (Wales) – was born in Pembrokeshire c.1146 and died c.1223. He made four visits to Ireland, in 1183, 1185, 1199 and 1204. Related to a number of the Norman lords who were involved in the invasion of Ireland, Gerald was a cleric and a writer of some significance. He wrote seventeen works, all in Latin, including *Topographia Hibernica (Topography of Ireland)*, the first significant written portrayal of Ireland by a foreign person who had visited the place. He also brought with him a certain breadth of European learning, having spent many years in Paris by the time he first set foot in Ireland. Having studied in France for over a decade, he became archdeacon of Brecon in 1175 and would have become bishop of St David's had not the king (Henry II) refused to appoint a Welshman to a see in Wales.

In 1184, however, Gerald became a member of Henry II's entourage, and it was with John (the king's son, to whom Gerald was tutor) that he visited Ireland a second time in 1185. Thus the *Topography* was drawn from Gerald's vision of Ireland in the mid-1180s, and it is an extremely valuable period piece for Irish historians. It is divided into three parts. In Gerald's own words:

> *The first part treats of the Position of Ireland ....*
> *The second part treats of the Wonders and Miracles of Ireland .... The third part treats of the Inhabitants of the Country.*

Gerald's work addresses itself respectively, therefore, to the *geographical*, the *remarkable*, and the *human/historical* – this third section looking at the history of Ireland from the 'first arrival' up to the twelfth century inhabitants. It is a text which has been the object of severe attacks. As historians, we must ask certain crucial questions regarding Gerald. Where did he go in Ireland during the visits upon which the *Topography* was based? What do his background and connections suggest regarding the views, the presuppositions which he would have brought to his writing? Above all, for whom and in what context was the work written?

On his first visit it is evident that he became familiar, to some degree, with the regions of Cork and Waterford – beyond that we do not know how far Gerald's experience reached. His second visit was more extensive. He certainly saw Waterford,

Meath, Kildare and Dublin, and was quite possibly also in Wicklow and the Athlone region. Much of the rest of the island was unknown to the Normans anyway. So his sight of Ireland was partial, though (particularly on his second trip) not insubstantial. As to his background and connections, it is important to recognise that Gerald was woven into a web of people instrumental in the twelfth century invasion of Ireland. His uncle, Maurice FitzGerald, was indeed one of the leaders of that invasion. Thus Gerald – if he is to be understood in an appropriate historical setting – must be seen as one surfing to Ireland on a wave of Norman incursion. As we have observed, his second visit to the island was in the company of Henry II's son, John, and Gerald actually dedicated the *Topography* to the king whose entourage he had joined in 1184. Indeed Gerald at times rather overdosed on eulogy where Henry was concerned:

> *The victories of Henry the Second,*
> *king of the English*
>
> *Your victories vie with the whole round of the world. Our western Alexander, you have stretched your arm from the Pyrenean mountains even to these far western bounds of the northern ocean. As many as are the lands provided by nature in these parts, so many are your victories. If the limits of your expeditions are sought – there will be no more of the world left for you before there will be an end to your activities. A courageous heart may find no lands to conquer. Your victories can never cease. Your triumphs cannot cease, but only that over which you may triumph.*

So Gerald's account has to be examined in its partisan context. What does he say of the late-twelfth-century Ireland which he encountered? Much of it is unflattering. 'It is only in the case of musical instruments' – he wrote – 'that I find any commendable diligence in the people. They seem to me to be incomparably more skilled in these than any other people that I have seen.' Rare praise, for he also claimed that Ireland's saints 'seem to be of a vindictive cast of mind' and that her inhabitants

> *are a wild and inhospitable people. They live on beasts only, and live like beasts. They have not progressed at all from the primitive habits of pastoral living.*

Indeed, Gerald's condemnation of the Irish was as merciless as it was generalised; 'above all other peoples' – he wrote – 'they always practise treachery. When they give their word to anyone, they do not keep it.'

Beyond such generalised abuse – and in addition to tales of bestiality in Connacht and Paris – Gerald does offer certain nuggets which must be judged of greater value to the historian. The third section of the work, in particular, presents useful insights regarding late-twelfth-century Irish people, since Gerald's account here must have relied heavily on the perceptions of people in Ireland. There emerges from his account a 'stages' view of Irish history, with different arrivals successively contributing to the population of the island. It is also intriguing that

St Canice's Cathedral, Kilkenny. The present structure dates from the thirteenth century, though it was modified in the seventeenth century and restored in the eighteenth and nineteenth centuries.

Gerald lays stress on there having been in Ireland a tradition of united kingship ('Slanius became the sole king of the whole of Ireland') though it should also be noted that he argued 'that Ireland can with some right be claimed by the kings of Britain'.

Kingship continued to be a crucial aspect of Irish society after the twelfth century invasion. This was true not only in Ireland. As the historian, J.R. Lander, put it, 'In the medieval and the early modern world

there was no substitute for a mature and vigorous king, for a king had to rule as well as reign'. If scepticism had to be applied regarding the claims of pre-invasion rulers in Ireland, what of the situation after 1169? In April 1172 Henry II concluded his Irish visit – the only one he was to make. Henry's performance in Ireland had been an impressive – albeit an intruding – one. What was the situation which he left behind him? On departing from Ireland Henry appointed Hugh de Lacy as justiciar (or administrator). De Lacy was now the representative of Henry's power in Ireland, and he was also granted Meath and appointed to specific authority over Dublin. Royal garrisons provided symbolic and practical evidence of Henry's rule, and soon after his departure Hugh de Lacy had emphasised his own strength by killing Tiernan O'Rourke, king of Breifne. But the English royal hold on Ireland was in fact far from total. This was tacitly stated by Henry in 1175 with the Treaty of Windsor between himself and Rory O'Connor. This agreement involved O'Connor yielding to Henry's authority in return for lordship over those regions which Henry had not been in a position to take over. Thus a formal division was recognised between Irish and English spheres of influence, and the pattern of incomplete conquest once again became evident.

In 1177 Henry bestowed on his son (John) the title 'Lord of Ireland'. But the struggle for control of Ireland was a continuing and contested one. Henry in fact reneged on the Treaty of Windsor, granting new lands to certain of his barons – behaviour reminiscent of that which Gerald of Wales had chauvinistically attributed to the Irish. Norman castles continued to sprout, and by the middle of the thirteenth century the Normans had come to control most of the island. Tir Conaill and Tir Eoghain in the north stood outside the conquest and Connacht was less densely affected than the east, but the Norman settlement was, nevertheless, a significantly successful one. The personnel soon changed: Strongbow died in 1176, Maurice FitzGerald (Gerald of Wales' uncle) in the same year, and Hugh de Lacy was killed ten years later. But the sea of Norman occupation remained. Indeed, the commitment to control over Ireland became, if anything, more resolute owing to the potential economic advantage to be derived from access to Irish agricultural land. Grants were followed by cultivation, as well as by defence, and the Normans introduced to the island a feudal system of land holding common not only in England but also throughout much of mainland Europe. In this instance, therefore, English rule in Ireland actually resulted in greater Irish conformity to European practice – a theme which was to recur, though more direct links between Ireland and Europe also continued. The feudal system, in essence, involved the king owning all the land but granting it out in return for allegiance and the provision of services or payments. At lower levels, too, there was a feudal relation, with major nobles dividing their land between less major nobles who themselves had tenants. Thus a pyramid of economically based allegiance took hold and, in a sense, this was reflected by the political change which Norman intrusion brought to Ireland. The justiciar headed the military, civil, and judicial structures, and was assisted by an influential council of officials. By the end of the thirteenth century local representatives were in fact being called to a parliament. This was primarily concerned with taxation, and although its influence was limited it is a further indication of the moves made under Norman rule towards a form of effective government. This should not be overplayed. The Normans' role in Ireland was a less all-embracing one than the one which they had played in England. It is as another layer in Ireland's past – admittedly an influential one – that the incoming Normans should be viewed. The twelfth century invasion was actually less of a straightforward fault line than has often been assumed. Precisely because there was no solid, central, governmental edifice of which they could assume possession, the Normans found their power in Ireland less universal than might otherwise have been the case. For the same reason, their moves towards the creation of governmental machinery should not casually be dismissed.

Another notable contribution was in the language spoken by the people. The creation of new towns was a significant and lasting aspect of invader culture – with Athlone, Galway and Kilkenny among those whose roots lie in Norman innovation – and it was in the towns of the eastern side of the island that linguistic change was most concentrated. Towns tended to be in a state of direct subjection to the crown, and so English became the spoken language. Other cultural changes also grew. Early Norman defences were towers, constructed of wood and situated on man-made mounds. But there quickly developed among the newcomers an understandable preference for sturdier fortifications, and between the late-twelfth century and the earlier part of the fourteenth century stone castles were built. A common design involved a central keep, often built into its surrounding walls. Such structures that have survived remain impressive even today, Carrickfergus Castle (to the north of Belfast) being a good example.

While such traces of Norman influence proved resilient, English rulers were distracted by other concerns from a more extensive conquest. It is also worth noting the toughness of will of the old Chieftains. Irish rulers continued to enjoy control in Connacht during much of the thirteenth century in the form of the O'Connors. In 1270 Aedh O'Connor scored a victory over an army led by Ralph d'Ufford (royal justiciar) and Walter de Burgo (who had become earl of Ulster in 1263). Walter's son, Richard, later became an influential figure in northern Ireland between 1286 and 1320. Under his influence English authority was to spread into Donegal. The picture of power in Ireland at this time was a complex one (involving a mixture of cooperation and coercion), with a variety of claimants to royal rule.

To complicate matters further, Edward Bruce invaded Ireland from Scotland in 1315, landing at Larne in the northeast of the country. The events preceding this invasion involve, in part, the conflict between England and Scotland. King Edward I, who ruled England at the end of the thirteenth and beginning of the fourteenth century, had enjoyed significant success in his efforts to conquer Welsh territory in the early 1280s. But his overtures in a Scottish direction met with less fruitful results. Inroads were made, but the conquest of Scotland remained elusive. By the time that Edward II became English king in 1307, Robert Bruce had emerged as a powerful leader of Scottish resistance to English advances. In 1314 the famous battle of Bannockburn saw Robert inflict a defeat on English forces, and it led to the Larne landing of 1315. Edward II had utilised human and other resources drawn from Ireland, and Robert Bruce held that an attack on Ireland might not only provide a kingdom for his brother, Edward, but might also help to dent English power in the process. Edward Bruce's expedition eventually failed, but not without first having achieved notable success. Edward – who had built alliances with a number of Irish leaders – defeated Richard de Burgo (earl of Ulster) at the battle of Connor in 1315 and was finally crowned king of Ireland in May 1316 at Faughart (county Louth).

English rule in Ireland was thus exposed as vulnerable – at least in the short term. The Scottish incursion also prompted at least one effort to undermine England's attempt to rule Ireland. When he arrived in Ireland in 1315 Edward Bruce had allied himself with the king of Tir Eoghain, Donal O'Neill. In 1317 O'Neill communicated with the pope, John XXII, asking he should back Edward's claims to Irish kingship. The arguments which O'Neill employed are interesting. For although it could not be claimed that he represented a united Irish people, his assertions embodied ideas of Irish freedom and of the illegitimacy of English claims on the island of Ireland. Prior to English intrusion, claimed O'Neill, the people in Ireland had been characterised by religious devotion and also by liberty; the Norman invasion which ended this situation had been wrongly

Facing page and overleaf:
Cahir Castle, County Tipperary, erected in the twelfth century on the River Suir.

sanctioned by Pope Adrian IV (who happened to be English). Not only was Adrian's Bull unacceptable in itself – O'Neill continued – but the subsequent actions of the English in Ireland would anyway have undermined the legitimacy of the conquest. For if the English were supposed to master Ireland in order to reform its church, then their role was a Christian one. Yet in reality, O'Neill's Irish Remonstrance maintained, the English had acted in a deeply unchristian spirit – rather than displaying a zeal to draw the Irish back to truly holy ways they had instead oppressed them. Thus English rule was not legitimate in Ireland, and the authority of a Scottish king had been supported in its place.

But although this document is a fascinating one it lacked both historical substance and practical effect. To suggest that the Irish people had been free, that their freedom had been impinged upon by twelfth century invasion, and that they had responded by seeking a Scottish alternative to English authority –

this would be to simplify the complex reality of Irish political life. To claim instead that the Irish peoples had been free, to recognise that the Norman invasion had in fact been greeted by a telling variety of responses from an equally telling variety of Irish rulers, and to admit that attitudes to the Bruce invasion had also been mixed – these responses would be more historically reliable. This is not to say that the twelfth century Norman incursion into Ireland was justified. It is merely to recognise that hints regarding a united Ireland are incorrect when applied to the time of the invasion. Whatever one makes of it Donal O'Neill's plea to the pope had little effect. The issue of Bruce's kingship was decided by force and without papal influence determining the outcome. In 1318 Edward Bruce was defeated and killed in battle at Faughart (not far from Dundalk) by a colonial force led by John de Bermingham.

The following year de Bermingham became earl of Louth, an example of the prevalent process of the

Right: *a conference between the Earl of Gloucester and an Irish chief during Richard II's campaign in Ireland.*

Below right: *Richard II knighting the four kings of Ireland – O'Neill, O'Connor, O'Brien and MacMurrough.*

Below: *Carrickfergus Castle, County Antrim. Following the Norman invasion stone castles were built for defence.*

de Burgo (earl of Ulster) pushed royal interests; but we should be cautious regarding the notion of effective Anglo-Irish authority in Ireland. In this period power was exercised in the context of a patchwork of claims to authority. And within this pattern there were clashes, such as that between the de Burgo and the FitzGerald factions.

There was a certain anxiety on the part of the royal authorities in the early fourteenth century regarding the way in which certain Norman nobles showed themselves prepared to team up with Gaelic leaders. Such alliances – it was held – threatened to undermine the power of the English king in Ireland. Edward III in 1361 gave his son, Lionel of Clarence, the role of king's lieutenant in Ireland, and this appointment led to the famous Statutes of Kilkenny, which emerged from a parliament held by Lionel in 1366. These statutes were addressed to the king's subjects and sought to ensure that, although the conquest of Ireland might be incomplete, there would nevertheless be a maintenance of a loyal, royally ruled, English-style part of the island of Ireland. Under the laws of 1366 it was enacted that English colonists should have no trade with the Irish, nor any marital or concubinary relations with them. They were not even allowed to have contact with Irish poets or musicians lest the artists should act as spies. It was further stated that colonists (and indeed the loyal Irish) should use only the English language, and that neither Marcher Law nor Irish (Brehon)

granting of privileges to Anglo-Irish nobles. Indeed, the attempted securing of England's Irish rule was an ongoing effort within which patronage played a crucial part. Edward III – king of England between 1327 and 1377 – stated early in the 1330s that he intended personally to visit Ireland. But this proposed trip never materialised, and in fact English royal rule of Ireland continued to be pursued by envoys sent by the king. Anthony Lucy (the justiciar) and William

Law should be observed. Irish people were to be given no religious rights. Wars between the English in Ireland were proscribed, as were privately pursued wars against the Irish. The Statutes of Kilkenny represented a development of earlier attempts to preserve the distinctively English quality of English Ireland. During the two decades which had preceded the Kilkenny parliament there had, for example, been efforts to control marriage between English and Irish partners and also to consolidate the use of English rather than of Irish law. Such moves testify to the degree to which Ireland's mid-fourteenth-century English population had immersed itself in Irishness. The Kilkenny laws of 1366 can be seen as a kind of legislative breathalyser, with those Anglo-Irish who did not conform being judged to have stepped over the acceptable limit and to have absorbed a dangerous quantity of Irishness.

Below left: *upper Lake Killarney, County Kerry.*

If the Statutes of Kilkenny point to certain concerns of the English authorities regarding Ireland, what of Gaelic political culture at this time? There was something of a reassertion both of hope and of influence by the native rulers, with lands and castles being taken from the colonisers by the Irish. The area controlled by the English colony shrunk during the fifteenth century. At the end of the previous century the English king, Richard II, had attempted to halt the sinking of the colonial ship in Ireland and had made two expeditions there. The first (in 1394) saw the king bring a large army and achieve some success in winning submission from Irish leaders. In 1399 Richard returned, but on this occasion a power struggle in England decided the issue. Henry of Derby claimed the English crown and, with Richard being compelled into abdication, Henry became King Henry IV. Thus Richard's efforts in Ireland were

Below: *Grace O'Malley's Castle on Clare Island, County Mayo.*

scuppered. The eastern portion of the island was the part in which royal rule was maintained, but this was a territorially small foothold. In the latter part of the century a defensive fortification was constructed to protect the Dublin-centred Pale, which was still subject to English royal authority. This area took in territory from counties Louth, Meath, Dublin and Kildare. But beyond this region lay most of the island, ruled over by a variety of native and Anglo-Irish lords. Neither group achieved anything like dominance over Ireland during this period. Indeed, the Anglo-Irish nobles held a pivotal position in terms of fifteenth century influence, and English government in Ireland relied on harmonious relations with these powerful figures. The earls of Desmond and of Kildare (both earldoms being held by branches of the FitzGerald family) enjoyed considerable strength, the Kildare House coming to prominence

with successive earls filling the position of chief governor of Ireland during the late-fifteenth and early-sixteenth centuries.

This kind of political stability was to be jolted during the crucial sixteenth century. Again it is possible to trace the tensions in the era preceding it. The reign of King Henry VIII (1509-47) was to witness the powerful reassertion of English royal rule in Ireland. But the tussle involving Henry's father (Henry VII, king of England between 1485 and 1509) and Garret More FitzGerald had already hinted at the direction which Anglo-Irish relations would later take. Born in the mid-fifteenth century, Garret More FitzGerald had become earl of Kildare in the 1470s. He became the most famous and the most powerful of the fifteenth century Anglo-Irish earls, and in 1487 he even supported the claims of Lambert Simnel

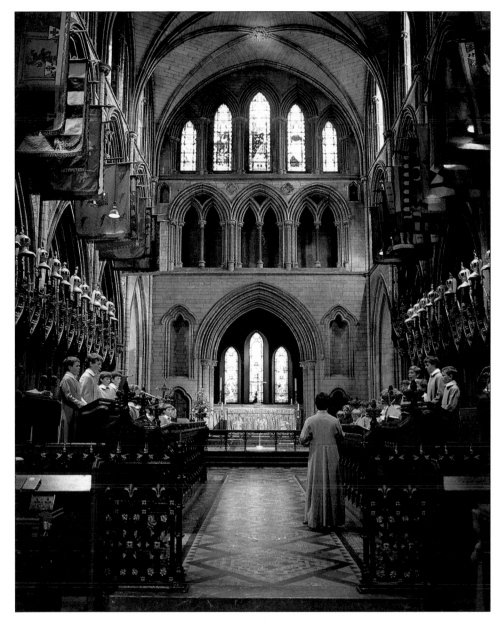

Above: *St Patrick's Cathedral, Dublin. According to legend, Patrick used to baptise on the site of this church.*

Facing page top right: *Ballylongford Cross, a late-fifteenth-century processional cross of gilt silver.*

Facing page bottom left: *King Henry VIII of England. His reign (1509-1547) saw the reassertion of English rule in Ireland.*

Ireland if they had royal licence to do so. It also stated that prior royal approval of all intended parliamentary legislation would in future be required. Thus, well before the death of the Great Earl in 1513 there were signs of a Tudor intention to take more control of Ireland. Too much should not be made of this, of course. There were huge differences – in personality as in policy and historical context between Henry VII and Henry VIII. But the Drogheda parliament of 1494 should certainly not be overlooked in our wide-angle appreciation of the history and politics of early modern Ireland.

Following Garret More FitzGerald's demise his son, Garret Og, became the ninth earl of Kildare and also the lord deputy of Ireland. During the 1530s Garret Og FitzGerald was called to London, and during his absence there occurred a rebellion which was directed at English authority and which was led by his son – Thomas FitzGerald, Lord Offaly. Better known to history as 'Silken Thomas', Lord Offaly's 1534 resistance to English authority in Ireland represented a restatement of Kildare strength, the message to Henry VIII being that English rule in Ireland depended on the House of Kildare. But in Henry VIII Thomas faced one to whom swaggering pride was far from alien, and in October 1534 William Skeffington's arrival in Ireland signalled the start of a process of suppression. Henry's appointment of Skeffington as deputy in Ireland was underlined militarily by the large force with which the new appointee was equipped. By 1535 Silken Thomas' Maynooth base had been taken, and the severity of the royal attitude was reflected in the killing of those who surrendered to the king's forces. Thomas himself was executed in London in 1537 and, as his father was also dead, the Kildare faction was left considerably weakened. The resistance of 1534 had resulted in the forceful reassertion of English authority in Ireland.

The reign of Henry VIII in England also brought religious reformation, resulting in a distinctively English form of Protestantism. The relationship between religion and political life rendered it vital that Henry's authority be recognised in the religious as in the temporal sphere. An Irish parliament met in 1536 under the new deputy, Lord Grey, and confirmed Henry as supreme head of the church. The English parliament had taken a similar step in the course of the king's messy break with Rome, and this Irish law reinforced through statute the power of the Tudor dynasty in Ireland. In the same year as this parliament had come together, George Browne was appointed archbishop of Dublin. During the following reign (that of Edward VI, 1547-53) Browne attempted to continue the process of pushing the cause of religious reform in Ireland. As in parts of England, however,

(whose pretensions to the English throne represented a challenge to the authority of Henry VII). Having resisted English efforts to remove him as justiciar, Garret was eventually arrested in 1495 and taken to London. Yet he was subsequently restored as justiciar by Henry VII, whose intelligent pragmatism led him to recognise the authority which Garret possessed in Ireland. In fact, up until his death in 1513 the 'Great Earl' cut an impressively authoritative figure.

But there was another element within this period – Edward Poynings. Sent to Ireland by Henry VII, Poynings called a parliament which met at Drogheda in 1494. This not only accused Garret More FitzGerald of treason, but also produced the measure with which Poynings' name has become lastingly and famously associated. 'Poynings' Law' decreed that future parliaments would only be able to meet in

IRELAND

there was some strong opposition to alterations regarding the Mass. As is so often the case, religious habit conflicted stubbornly with attempts at theological change. But the reformation, once planted in Ireland, proved to have sturdy roots. In part this was due to extremely worldly considerations – not even the passionately Catholic Mary Tudor (queen of England between 1553 and 1558) embarked, for example, on the restoration of monastic land and property which had been dissolved as part of the reformation process.

What of other areas of Irish administration? The undermining of the Kildare interest led to certain problems for English rule. Certain Gaelic nobles challenged the people of the Pale by means of raids. The government replied in kind via military missions and also by means of garrisoning the edges of the Pale. In the end, however, Silken Thomas was perhaps proved right, with the Geraldine heir having his title and some of his lands returned to him. In contrast, Gaelic rulers of the Irish midlands – over whom the Kildare House had enjoyed a certain dominance in the past – again lost out, being dispossessed and shunted west. There was an option available, but it was a humiliating one which involved being on the receiving end of serious cultural and political bullying. Gaelic rulers could obtain the recognition and support of the English monarch if they acknowledged that monarch to be their legitimate ruler. But the process went beyond this. The Gaelic leaders were also to abandon military practices – an important concession from the English point of view – and to further the process of extending English administration within the Gaelic-controlled areas.

In 1541 an Irish parliament had confirmed England's King Henry VIII as king also of Ireland. In the decade after Henry VIII's death there were further steps taken to entrench the English influence in Ireland, with lands seized in the counties of Laois and Offaly being provided for settlement by people from England or from the English Pale in Ireland. But no all-Ireland effective government emerged at this point, and the story remained one of partial control and of varying political cultures.

The last in the sequence of Tudor monarchs, Elizabeth I, came to power in 1558. Elizabeth sought to continue the development of an English form of Protestantism. In 1560 an Irish parliament confirmed her position as head of the Irish church – again, the importance of religion in affairs of state should be stressed. A further piece of legislation pressed upon clergy the Elizabethan *Book of Common Prayer* (which revised the 1552 book) and although there was comparatively little practical religious persecution under Elizabeth I, it should nevertheless be noted that objection to Tudor rule and objection to

Left: *Sir Walter Raleigh (c1552-1618), one of several important Elizabethans to go to Ireland following the sixteenth-century conquest by England.*

Facing page: *Elizabeth I, queen of England from 1558 to 1603. She encountered resistance to her rule in Ireland.*

Protestantism undoubtedly became intermingled.

There was certainly resistance to Elizabethan rule in Ireland. Ulster proved resilient, with the successive military efforts advocated by Thomas Radcliffe (earl of Sussex) failing to have their desired effect. In 1569 there was further trouble for the English rulers when James Fitz Maurice FitzGerald was among the leaders of a rebellion which had arisen in response to claims made on land in the possession of the FitzGeralds and the Butlers. Peter Carew had been the claimant. But he was only one of a number of English adventurers who had participated in a scheme sponsored by Henry Sidney, who became governor of Ireland during the 1560s. Sidney proposed taking lands from Gaelic owners who had militarily opposed the English monarch, or from those whose land was held not to be their own but rather to be the legitimate property of the English crown. The hostility of people such as James Fitz Maurice FitzGerald can hardly be judged to have been one of Irish history's most surprising phenomena. In the event James' rebellion was not successful and he fled to the European mainland. A decade later he returned with an avowed aim of fighting on behalf of the Catholic faith. Equipped with a papal ambassador and a small military body composed of Italians and Spaniards, FitzGerald was again unsuccessful. But prior to defeat there had

been notable backing for this venture – particularly in the south – and it was with a sizeable force and considerable brutality that Elizabeth responded to this challenge.

Following the suppression of this rebellion there emerged an extensive English settlement on confiscated land. Important trends can be detected in this episode. Religious undertones are evident in the rebellion and also in the subsequent plantation, for with settlement came a strengthening of Protestant Ireland (in Munster, at least). Also traceable in the 1569 and 1579 revolts is the cycle of rebellion following provocation. Implicit here is the attempted furtherance of the English hold on Ireland, and yet

Below: *Muckross Abbey, Killarney, County Kerry. Founded in the mid fifteenth century for the Franciscan order, this is one of Ireland's finest Gothic cathedrals.*

even after the settlements English control of Ireland was far from complete.

One further feature of this rebellious sequence of events was the European connection. Not for the last time mainland European players were to be involved in conflict between Irish challengers and the English government. A European dimension of a different kind entered Irish history during the 1580s, with Anglo-Spanish hostilities resulting in the famous but unsuccessful Armada. Certain of those Spanish ships which had not been destroyed in this celebrated defeat looked to the Irish west coast to provide refuge. The fate of those crew members who made it safely to land reflected the political variations in Ireland. Little mercy awaited Spaniards except in the province of Ulster, most of which had managed to evade Tudor advances. Yet English governmental ambitions in the Elizabethan period included the aim of bringing Ulster into the English political orbit. The consensus among the English administrators appears to have been to pursue the aim of breaking up the territory, even if considerable influence were to be left with the O'Neill dynasty.

O'Neill authority represented the major problem for English government in this region of Ireland, and the toughest incarnation of this authority was Hugh O'Neill, who had become earl of Tyrone in 1585. O'Neill's career illuminates some of the complications of early modern Irish history. Born in 1550, he was the heir to the baron of Dungannon, Matthew O'Neill, whose inheritance of the earldom of Tyrone was

contested and who never realised his claim. Indeed, Hugh O'Neill's accession to the earldom grew out of his immersion in English culture and politics. After his grandfather (Conn O'Neill, first earl of Tyrone) had died, Hugh had been taken to England and put through the process of an English lord's education. Returning to Ireland in the 1560s, it was as a result of his loyal service to Elizabeth that he was given the Tyrone earldom. Having acted in shrewd collusion with English allies in opposition to his dynastic competitors in Ulster, O'Neill then set himself more ambitious aims than English administrators were prepared to accept. He sought to regain the whole lordship of Tyrone, and during the last decade of the sixteenth century tension brewed between this talented soldier and the English authorities. In 1595 Hugh embarked on rebellion and, with his ally Red Hugh O'Donnell (from Tyrconnell), he made overtures seeking Spanish assistance. Another ingredient of the continental dimension can again be tasted here. O'Neill's military success in 1598 at the battle of the Yellow Ford demonstrated his potential. Indeed, the Spanish king, Philip III, provided Hugh with an army which landed at Kinsale in 1601. O'Neill, O'Donnell and their continental comrades were, however, severely beaten by the forces of the government. The battle of Kinsale was followed by further resistance on O'Neill's part, but in 1603 – just days after the death of Elizabeth I – Hugh surrendered. Sturdy Gaelic opposition had eventually been overcome by English power.

CHAPTER THREE

PLANTATION AND PATRIOTISM

1603 – 1800

*It is therefore our business carefully to cultivate in our minds,
to rear to the most perfect vigour and maturity, every sort of
generous and honest feeling that belongs to our nature. To bring
the dispositions that are lovely in private life into the service
and conduct of the commonwealth; so to be patriots,
as not to forget we are gentlemen.*

EDMUND BURKE

Hugh O'Neill's challenge had been a major one. His defeat was correspondingly significant, and important changes were indeed to occur in the wake of this turbulent episode. In 1607 – four years after his surrender – Hugh and many other Ulster lords opted for voluntary exile in Europe, O'Neill himself dying in Rome nine years later. To the administrators of English rule in Ireland the lesson was that Gaelic, Catholic lords were a dangerous breed as far as crown rule was concerned. Things were not quite this simple, however, for there appears also to have been a measure of concern regarding the reliability of the Old English nobles – those whose ancestors had pioneered the Anglo-Norman conquest of Ireland. The insecurity of the English hold which is highlighted by these attitudes galvanised the authorities into measures aimed at securing English rule. Another pivotal point in Irish history had therefore been reached.

Following the 'flight of the earls' to Europe in 1607 the English government was given a chance to consolidate its strength in Ireland. James I had followed Elizabeth on the English throne in 1603 and, like her, he included Ireland among his monarchical possessions. The lord deputy in Ireland – Arthur Chichester – took six of Ulster's nine counties after the fleeing earls' territory had been declared forfeit to the English monarchy. In 1609 the Articles of Plantation emerged, facilitating a process of settlement which brought Scottish and English people to the island. Some land was also allotted to Irish people, though these landlords were obliged to farm according to English practice. The bullying nature of the plantation process and the dispossession of the Irish cannot be morally condoned simply because it appeared to be tactically sensible. But the variation of settlement patterns should be noted, particularly as the shapes of later Irish political life were beginning here to be moulded. It was in eastern Ulster that the process of colonisation took firmest root. Counties Antrim and Down witnessed the fiercest example, with Scottish Protestant immigration resulting in the forcible uprooting of Irish Catholic natives. Already one can trace the emerging characteristics of northern Irish political history. It was not merely a case of dispossessor and dispossessed, nor solely one of Protestant and Catholic, or of Scottish versus Irish; the politics of this region derived from the fact that all three distinctions were relevant. Religion, ethnicity and the process of plantation combined to produce a most significant and resilient cultural fault line.

The situation in county Londonderry was different, however, from that in south Antrim or north Down. Insufficient numbers of Scottish or English people could be drawn to Londonderry, and

Previous pages: *the Mountains of Mourne, near Tollymore Forest Park in County Down.*

Above: *Oliver Cromwell (1599-1658), infamous for the violence against Drogheda and Wexford in 1649.*

Facing page: *King Charles' fort, Kinsale, County Cork, built by the Duke of Ormond in the late seventeenth century.*

so Irish tenants formed an important part of the new picture there. More broadly, plantation also affected many other parts of seventeenth-century Ireland, including Carlow, Leitrim, Longford and Wexford. In every Irish county, indeed, there came to be at least some landowners who originated from the neighbouring island. Englishness, in fact, was seriously in vogue, to the extent of some of the native landowners stepping down the road toward the emulation of things Anglo. English power brought with it a coercive logic tending in the direction of assimilation. Linguistic, sartorial, architectural and legal developments reflected as much.

During the 1630s a significant development in Anglo-Irish politics was heralded by the appointment of Thomas Wentworth as lord deputy. Later to become the earl of Strafford, Wentworth embarked on a rigorous policy of attempting to increase royal revenue and also royal power in Ireland. Once again the tensions of English political life had an important bearing on Irish affairs. Charles I (king of England between 1625 and 1649) experienced increasing problems during the 1630s, and this decade in English politics exported some of its turbulence to Ireland. Wentworth's espousal of Laudianism represents an important example here. William Laud – archbishop of Canterbury from 1633 – was zealous for the enforcement of uniformity within the Church of England. But Wentworth's assumption of religious authority in Ireland alienated many in Ireland's English community. Similarly, his failure to grant promised concessions to Catholics generated irritation, while his harsh line on Ulster – with people being punished for their non-adherence to the 1609 Articles of Plantation – caused further resentment still. Hostility to Wentworth, therefore, was widespread in Ireland, and the next stage in the English crisis also influenced Irish experience in significant ways.

The year 1642 witnessed the start of the English civil war. The preceding year has achieved a high place in Irish history. In Ulster certain people within the Catholic land-owning class sought advancement of their interests through the medium of force. A number of local risings resulted in a combination of humiliation, expulsion and killing directed at recent settlers in the region. But Ulster was not the only scene of revolt in 1641. Rory O'More – whose family had suffered as a consequence of plantation in county Laois – colluded with Phelim O'Neill in his plan to subvert the government in Dublin. An attempt to take control of Dublin Castle failed, but the rebellion was not to be snuffed out so easily.

The rebels declared that they had the support of King Charles I and an alliance was forged between the Old English in Ireland and the native Irish.

Cracks began to show quickly enough between the partners in this intriguing relationship. But the strength of religious identification is unmistakable none the less. Catholics, though massively different in other ways, united as Catholics in the face of Protestant adversaries. Religious vision clearly meant much to these adversaries as well. When the English response to events in 1640s Ireland finally came, it turned out to be a cruel one. In a history peopled with simplistically portrayed goodies and baddies, Oliver Cromwell has tended to be placed among the latter group. Charles I had been executed in January 1649, and seven months later Cromwell arrived in Ireland, enjoying both civil and military authority. The English civil war had gone very badly for the Irish. In 1642 leading representatives of Catholic Ireland had gathered in Kilkenny, and tied their colours to the king's mast. There were stresses within this Catholic grouping, reflected by respective attitudes to Owen Roe O'Neill. Nephew of Hugh O'Neill, Owen Roe had spent considerable time in the Spanish army in a Europe which was experiencing the Thirty Years War. In 1642 O'Neill agreed to lead Ulster's rebels. But the fragility of the alliance can be gauged by the fact that Old English Catholics were reluctant to give O'Neill the backing he needed in the Ulster theatre of war. For O'Neill's approach involved the belief that Irish chiefs should try to rid Ireland of English power. The Old English, however, were less enthusiastic about severing links with the crown.

Whether they were thoroughly hostile to English rule or keen on royal reconciliation, the rebels were perceived by Cromwell in a fully negative light. Parliament had won the day in the civil war and Irish Catholic affection for crown authority was hardly likely to win friends in post-monarchical England. Cromwell was determined to avenge the slaughter of Protestants which had taken place in the early part of the decade. He also wished to restore English order to unruly Ireland, and to stamp on the head of any Irish remnants of royalism. In September 1649 the violence began, carried out by a tough military machine. Drogheda was attacked and, following its refusal to surrender, the garrison was killed by Cromwell's forces. A similarly atrocious procedure occurred in October at Wexford. Military suppression succeeded in bringing about the defeat of the Irish. Cromwell himself departed from the island in 1650. Henry Ireton then acted as the enforcer, followed after his death by Charles Fleetwood. Between these two, English military command was effectively exercised by Edmund Ludlow, and this succession of figures – Cromwell, Ireton, Ludlow, Fleetwood – oversaw the defeat of Irish resistance.

But the mission went beyond the eradication of

Above: *the Long Room in Thomas Burgh Library, Trinity College, Dublin, which houses the famous Book of Kells.*

Left: *Trinity College, Dublin. Founded in 1592 by Queen Elizabeth I, Trinity is a world-famous centre of learning.*

Right: *the Campanile in the charming quadrangle of Trinity College, Dublin.*

Irish military potential. Protestant conversion might not have been foremost in the mind during the carnage at Drogheda or Wexford. But Protestantisation was none the less part of the overall vision for Ireland. It was also part of the less than grand design that Catholic lands should be confiscated. The English parliament in 1652 passed an Act of Settlement which facilitated the taking of land from owners who had not demonstrated their loyalty during the years of the rebellion. Many soldiers were rewarded with such forfeited lands. Catholics were forced to take land in Connacht. Thus the 1640s and 1650s present a painful and all too familiar pattern – rebellion mingled with a search for revenge;

severe reaction by those in authority; massacres; economic and religious marginalisation; the creation of myths portraying the viciousness and treachery of one's opponents – these features overlay one another and represent a complicated catalogue of bloody and ugly conflict.

Cromwell's reputation in Ireland continued well after his death; non-monarchical rule in England did not. He died in 1658, and within two years Charles II was king of England, Scotland and Ireland. But the Irish parliament which met in 1661 was heavily Cromwellian in complexion. In 1662 an Act of Settlement facilitated claims from those who had not been guilty of rebellion, regarding lands of which

Right: *Sir William Petty (1623-1687), author of* The Political Anatomy of Ireland *and founder of the Dublin Philosophical Society in 1683.*

Below: *the Battle of the Boyne – fought in July 1690 between the forces of William of Orange and James II of England.*

they had been dispossessed. But in practice widespread re-transfer did not occur. The 1665 Act of Explanation attempted to compensate Protestants who had lost land returned to Catholics. Although some Catholics did regain land, Catholic land grievance remained. At the start of the 1640s Catholics had held over half of the land in Ireland. But in the 1660s the picture was very different. In the period after the Act of Explanation, Catholics held less than a quarter of Irish land. Thus religious difference was carved into patterns of land ownership.

Late-seventeenth-century Catholicism made ground in terms of organisation and control. The Church of Ireland also made progress, enjoying land restoration and a strengthening of its hierarchy. Variety rather than uniformity persisted, a trend emphasised by the continued vitality of northern Presbyterianism. The Church of Ireland was the officially established church. If numbers provided an index of potential, then it was the Catholic tradition which had most to anticipate. In a sense this proved to be the case. This process took time to develop, but there were hopes of great things among sections of the Catholic population when, in 1685, the Catholic James II came to the throne. It was assumed by many that land and influence would surely follow. Certain changes did take place. An eminent Irish Catholic, Richard Talbot, was given the title Earl of Tyrconnell in 1685. He took charge of the army and reorganised it with an infusion of Catholic blood. Catholics became judges and came to sit on the Privy Council, and when Talbot became lord deputy in 1687 Protestant anxiety increased still further. Such fear could only be rendered even more acute by consideration of Talbot's determination that the Cromwellian confiscations of land be undone.

In fact the reign of James II was a short one. Although he lived until 1701 he was driven from power in 1688, to be succeeded the following year by William III and Mary II as king and queen of England. In 1689, James II landed in Ireland from France. His Scottish followers having been beaten in battle, Ireland appeared to offer James a last chance to regain power. But events unfolded unhappily for the ousted ruler. Londonderry had stood against James' supporters and a famous siege failed to break the resilient town. William III landed in Ireland in June 1690. The following month witnessed the battle of the Boyne, where Protestant William gained the day over Catholic James. The religious labels are all too tragically relevant here. While the conflict between William and James was in one sense an English contest decided in Ireland, it reflected very Irish realities. James had called in 1689 a predominantly Catholic parliament. The Act of Settlement was repealed – further evidence of the vital significance

of land in Irish political consciousness. Those who had held land in 1641 were now able to seek restitution of losses incurred in the Cromwellian period.

This Dublin 'patriot' parliament was prevented from producing effective legislation by military reality. Because religion overlapped with questions such as land ownership it was a forceful phenomenon. The situation by 1689-90 was one in which the religious boundary reigned supreme. Religion, politics and economics were woven together in this period. The interrelation of these crucial factors underlines the integral importance of late-seventeenth-century Irish religious identification: it was present in all spheres of contemporary life.

Following the clash at the river Boyne James left for France. But the conflict continued after his departure. William also left Ireland in 1690, Patrick Sarsfield's Limerick Jacobites having repulsed the king's forces. But the absence of the figureheads did not remove the violence. In 1691 the Williamites took Athlone and inflicted defeat on their enemies at Aughrim. Eventually Sarsfield agreed to a treaty. Like the battles of Aughrim and the Boyne, the Treaty of Limerick has become lodged in Ireland's complex historical memory. Signed on 3 October 1691, it gave Irish soldiers a variety of choices, including the most popular one of going to France. It also provided for a measure of toleration where Ireland's Catholics were concerned. But it would be naive to attribute too great a role in 1690s political culture to the practice of religious toleration. The year 1695 saw the emergence of parliamentary acts which restricted Catholic rights regarding education and the bearing of arms. Parliament also legislated – in 1697 – for the banishment of Catholic clergy. So the flavour of the 1690s was a religiously sour one. The Penal Laws characterised the attitude of the victorious powerful. This attitude should not be condoned. But it was wholly predictable none the less. The 1640s and the 1680s had each, in their respective ways, instilled a measure of fear into the Protestant culture which thrived after the Williamite triumph.

In 1704 – two years after the accession to the English throne of Queen Anne (1702-14) – the penal legislation was extended with the introduction of restrictions on Catholic land-holding rights and on Catholic participation in public office. Prior to Anne's arrival on the throne legislation had gone some way toward directing Irish economic development in accordance with English designs. In 1696 Irish linen manufacture was encouraged, while in 1699 Irish woollen exports were restricted. Thus the English exertion of influence over Irish affairs represented self-defensive muscle-flexing on the part of the powerful. To non-Catholics in Ireland the bitter

history of the post-1640 period told its own tale –
Catholics were a threat to your property, position
and even to your life. Members of the Dublin
parliament represented a centre of enthusiasm for
penal legislation directed against Catholics. But to
the English authorities, too, there was a recognition
of the special position of the Roman Catholic religion
in Ireland. Even James II – hero of the Catholic cause
– appreciated the politically different implications
of Irish as opposed to English Catholicism.

And here we come to the really distinctive aspect
of the appalling penal measures in Ireland. For
religiously punitive legislation was not an unknown
phenomenon in contemporary Europe. The
distinguishing feature of the Irish case was that here
it was a religious majority rather than a minority
which was experiencing suppression. The penal
process could not realistically be hoped to convert
the Catholic population of Ireland to the Protestant
faith. At the root of the process was the intention that
Catholics should be kept down and out of positions
of influence. Excluded from parliament, the legal
profession, the armed or governmental services,
Catholics were the victims more of a structure of
repression than one of attempted conversion. It
should, however, be noted that many Catholics of
higher social status did make the required shift into
Protestant respectability. This was important, for

Above: *the Guinness Brewery, Dublin. Arthur Guinness bought the St James's Gate brewery in 1759.*

Left: *Arthur Guinness (1725-1803), the brewer, a Protestant who founded the first Sunday School in Ireland.*

Above left: *a beautiful Georgian doorway, one of many for which Dublin is renowned.*

Right: *the Customs House, Dublin, designed by James Gandon (1743-1820).*

Left: *Theobald Wolfe Tone (1763-1798), a republican who declared 'The great object of my life has been the independence of my country.'*

grievance until the early-nineteenth century. And land, as always, focused the fears of the powerful and the resentment of the marginalised. In the early-eighteenth century Irish Catholics represented approximately three-quarters of the island's population. Yet they owned only a tiny fraction of the land.

The second point worth adding to this discussion of penal pressure concerns Dissenters. Northern Irish Presbyterianism was a vibrant force in this period, but was officially penalised in certain ways. For religious discrimination was really a pro-Church of Ireland mechanism. The Dissenter tradition had less to complain about than did the Catholic one with which it was eventually to lock vicious horns. A parliamentary act of 1704 made it obligatory that those holding public office should take the sacrament according to Church of Ireland practice. Thus Presbyterians, too, were on the receiving end of discrimination. Even when the 1719 Toleration Act liberated Protestant Dissenters from the requirement of attending the services of the established church, their obligation to pay tithes still remained. Thus

instance, if a wealthy Catholic wanted his land to be passed on intact to one son. Only a Protestant could inherit in such a way. If conversion did not take place then the land would be divided up among the various male heirs, rather than going in one piece to the eldest. The application of this mechanism would ensure the subdivision of Catholic holdings, and would plainly bring about a decline in Catholic landed influence.

The Penal Laws will not be forgotten, but in order fully to understand their operation two further points should be made. First, a distinction should be drawn between the passing of legislation and the effective implementation of the laws so enacted. There was, in fact, considerable variation in the application of penal legislation in Ireland. The ban on Catholic arms-bearing, for example, soon lapsed into disuse, and the laws which impinged on practices of religious worship came increasingly to have little impact. There was greater alertness regarding those elements of the code which were seen as truly vital to the maintenance of Protestant ascendancy. Exclusion from parliament was to remain an important

Above: *George Berkeley (1685-1753), Bishop of Cloyne and a philosopher whose writings included* The Principles of Human Knowledge *and* The Querist.

Facing page bottom:
Edmund Burke (1729-1797), a famous orator and politician whose Reflections on the Revolution in France *was first published in 1790.*

Good pasture land facilitated the emergence of a prospering body of farmers in parts of Munster and Leinster – a development less common in the west of Ireland. In rural regions the role of the infamous absentee landlords, whose estates were leased and subdivided in their absence, has been the focus of much debate. But to attribute too much blame to non-resident aristocrats exempts from blame many rural actors lower down the social league table who were themselves happy to thrive at the expense of Ireland's poor. The pasture-farming class is one example. Domestic graziers became the focus of rural resentment later in Ireland's history, when the landlord class had been effectively bought out.

The relation between politics and economy was an intimate one. England's political hold on Ireland was reflected in the 1720 Declaratory Act, which recognised the right of the parliament at Westminster to legislate for Ireland. Prior to the passing of this act there had emerged and disappeared sophisticated commentators on Anglo-Irish relations. William Molyneux (1656-98) was educated at Trinity College, Dublin, and in addition to his contributions to the world of Irish philosophy he also had political experience as Member of Parliament for Dublin University during the 1690s. His pamphlet, *The Case of Ireland's being Bound by Acts of Parliament in England Stated* (1698), grew out of his consideration of the consequences of English laws for Irish industrial life. Molyneux's argument is important in representing a particular kind of 'national' sentiment. His argument effectively pointed in a nationalistic direction. But it is crucial to stress that to the Anglo-Irish, seventeenth-century mind of William Molyneux the Irish nation was the Protestant Irish nation. Given the modern day identification of Irish nationalism with the Catholic tradition, this is worth stating. The Protestant Ascendancy was precisely that, an ascendancy based on an exclusive definition of the nation.

The more famous Jonathan Swift (1667-1745) also paid attention to questions of English power and Irish economic life. Born in Dublin, Swift was educated at Kilkenny Grammar School and then (like Molyneux) at Trinity College, Dublin. In the 1690s he was ordained and in 1713 he became the Dean of Dublin's St Patrick's Cathedral (a position he held right up until 1745). Swift deserves consideration alongside Molyneux, for they both espoused a form of constitutional Irish independence. Swift's anonymous pamphlet from 1720 advocated the use of Irish manufactures, as did his *Drapier's Letters*, published in 1724. In these he opposed the supposed right of an Englishman, William Wood, to mint copper coins for use in Ireland. The patent in question had been granted to the duchess of Kendal and had

distinctions within Irish Protestantism – which have often been underestimated by observers – can clearly be detected within this era.

What of the eighteenth century economy? As noted, the parliament in London helped to direct the development of Irish trade (though it should be noted, for example, that in 1699 legislation aimed at limiting Irish export of woollens was passed in the Irish as well as the English parliament). Irish brewing underwent expansion; this trend was hampered by the parliamentary decision that hops could only be imported into Ireland from Britain. The linen industry was to flourish (especially in Ulster) following the encouragement which it received. Thus Irish economic developments generally followed an Anglo-friendly pattern.

Below: *Killala harbour, County Mayo. The village was occupied by the French during the politically turbulent year of 1798.*

Right: *Kilcummin village, County Mayo, the site of the French landing in 1798. Despite French involvement the 1798 rebellion failed.*

Facing page: *the Old Charitable Institute, Clifton House, Belfast, built in 1771.*

been bought by Wood, who had hoped to make a significant profit from the project. In 1723, however, the Irish parliament protested against the scheme and in the end, with Swift's prodding, the plan was abandoned.

Swift's witty brilliance excels within this Ascendancy tradition of Irish patriotism. But the Ascendancy intelligentsia had other heroes to offer to posterity, among them the orator Edmund Burke (1729-97), and the philosopher George Berkeley (1685-1753). Berkeley's assertion that truth was 'the game of the few' might perhaps be applied also to Irish politics in the latter part of the eighteenth century. For these were highly elitist times. Two charismatic figures were influential in differing ways during the late-eighteenth century: Henry Grattan and Theobald Wolfe Tone. Born in 1746, Grattan was educated at Trinity College, Dublin, and during the 1770s was called to the Irish Bar and entered the Irish parliament. His oratorical gifts brought him quickly to prominence, and he emerged as leader of the 'patriot' party, an opposition group in the Dublin parliament. The patriots sought and gained greater Irish independence from England. But the nature of this independence was limited. Grattan campaigned for the removal of the remaining restrictions on Irish commerce and for Irish legislative independence. The achievement of these two goals represented an important development in Irish political history. But 'Grattan's parliament' (as the 1782-1800 Dublin body came to be known) had legislative independence under the crown. It was not absolute independence from England that Grattan and his colleagues sought; it was autonomy within an English orbit.

Above: *the execution of Protestant prisoners at Wexford on 20th June 1798 during the rebellion. 'MWS' stands for 'Murder Without Sin'.*

Below: *a commemoration in Enniscorthy, County Wexford, of the 1798 Battle of Vinegar Hill. The rebellion of 1798 became an important part of Irish nationalist tradition.*

Above: *the battle of Vinegar Hill during the rebellion of 1798.*

opposed the parliamentary union with Britain which emerged in that year, he none the less sat in the union parliament in London between 1805 and 1820. Parliament was his natural medium. A leading member of the Protestant Ascendancy himself, Grattan nevertheless argued – with typical rhetorical flourish – that 'the Irish Protestant could never be free till the Irish Catholic had ceased to be a slave'. In the early-nineteenth century in the London parliament he espoused the cause of Catholic emancipation.

This issue of religious toleration brings us on to our second late-eighteenth-century focal figure. Theobald Wolfe Tone was born in 1763 and, like Grattan, he attended Trinity College, Dublin. Like Grattan, too, he pursued legal studies, but the two men were in fact highly different. Tone's *Argument on Behalf of the Catholics of Ireland* (1791) reflected his political enthusiasm, and later in the year he was involved in the foundation of the United Irishmen in Belfast. This movement began as a debating society with reform on its mind. But Tone and the United Irishmen are inescapably linked in historical memory with the rebellion – or rebellions – of 1798. Tone's ideology developed into a dreamy blend of republican separatism and religious tolerance, his thinking classically epitomised in seductive rhetoric:

> *(1796:) To subvert the tyranny of our execrable government, to break the connection with England, the never failing source of all our political evils, and to assert the independence of my country – these were my objects. To unite the whole people of Ireland, to abolish the memory of all past dissensions, and to substitute the common name of Irishman, in the place of the denominations of Protestant, Catholic and Dissenter – these were my means.*

> *(1798:) The great object of my life has been the independence of my country ... looking upon the connexion with England to have been her bane I have endeavoured by every means in my power to break that connexion ....*

But the events that actually materialised in 1798 deviated in many ways from the envisaged pattern. For one thing the rebellion failed; Tone's arrival with French forces could not alter the outcome and he himself was captured and sentenced to death before in fact committing suicide. In addition to this, the violence of 1798 took on a sectarian aspect in various places – precisely the division which Tone had sought to eradicate from Irish life. As so often in Irish experience, rhetoric and enthusiasm had an undeniable impact without bringing about the changes at which they were in fact directed.

Still, the achievements of 1782 should not be sneered at. In June the Declaratory Act (which had recognised the right of the London parliament to legislate for Ireland) was repealed. In July Poynings' Law was amended. As we saw earlier, this law had stated that Irish parliaments could only meet if they had royal licence to do so, and stipulated the necessity of prior royal approval for Irish parliamentary legislation. Now, however, the situation was to be different. After 1782 a royal right of veto remained, but not a right to alter Irish legislation. Henry Grattan was a thorough parliamentarian. In the words of the historian, Roy Foster, he was 'a quintessential "patriot" in being a good House of Commons man, with moderately conservative instincts'. Grattan's parliamentary instincts were not only evident in his pursuit of Irish parliamentary independence, but were further reflected in his career after 1800. Having

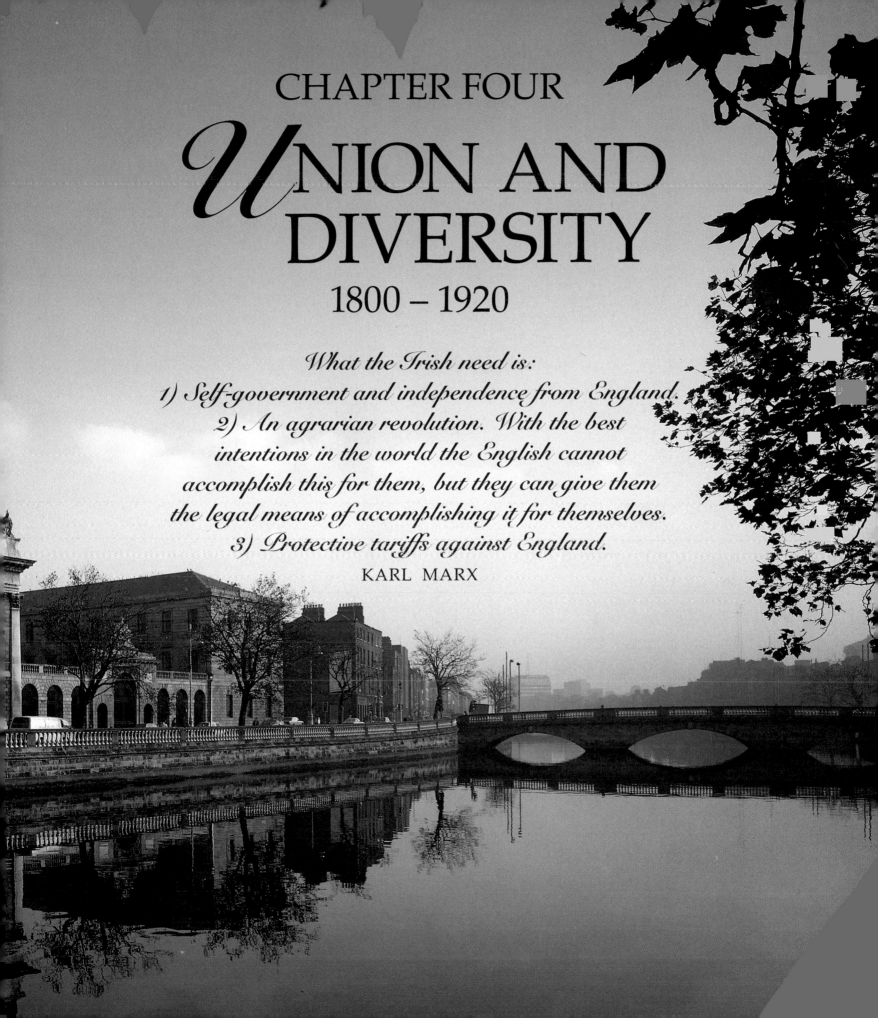

CHAPTER FOUR

UNION AND DIVERSITY

1800 – 1920

What the Irish need is:
1) Self-government and independence from England.
2) An agrarian revolution. With the best
intentions in the world the English cannot
accomplish this for them, but they can give them
the legal means of accomplishing it for themselves.
3) Protective tariffs against England.

KARL MARX

The cult of Theobald Wolfe Tone was to become a resilient one, with his being celebrated (or condemned) as the founding father of modern Irish republicanism. This description is a dangerous one. Yet in a way Tone has indeed been a figure for apostles of the Irish republic to celebrate. For later republican thought and practice were to reflect themes associated with Wolfe Tone. Separatist zeal; romantic conceptions of nationhood; vain aspirations to cross-sectarian unity; effective rhetoric; the rather less effective use of violence; striking commitment, even unto death; indulgence in political simplification; a good measure of Anglophobia – each of these elements was to recur in subsequent Irish republican experience and in this sense Tone's celebrated status is fitting.

More immediately, the rebellion with which he is associated helped convince the prime minister, William Pitt, of the need for a union between Ireland and Great Britain. Thus 'Grattan's parliament' was brought to an end. The Act of Union which passed through the Irish parliament in 1800 came into effect at the start of January 1801. The century which began in this way witnessed the development in Ireland of mutually hostile political and cultural traditions. Indeed, the persistence of conflict in modern Ireland owes much to this phenomenon – the simultaneous validity of apparently contradictory stances.

In practical terms, what did the Union involve? The United Kingdom of Great Britain and Ireland was reflected, in parliamentary terms, in a Westminster body at which Ireland had representatives. Certain importantly distinctive elements remained in the realm of Irish government after 1800; Ireland was not simply absorbed indiscriminately into the British political world. Financially there was Irish difference, and the vice-regal and Castle structures – so important before the Union – remained. The Union was certainly important. But in a sense it reflected rather than created Irish reality. Ironically, the degree of post-1800 continuity is evident even among those who were looking for drastic change. Brother of an eminent United Irishman, Robert Emmet (1778-1803) led an unsuccessful rebellion in 1803 and was subsequently hanged. Thus the United Irish connection lived on, and physical force earned a place in the history of the early nineteenth century, just as it had done at the end of the eighteenth. The significance of violence was eventually to be elevated to sophisticated heights. But in the early nineteenth century it was the emergence of a very different tradition which dominated the agenda.

Daniel O'Connell (1775-1847) came to be known as 'The Liberator', but 'the mobiliser' might be a more appropriate historical nickname. It was under

Previous pages: *the Four Courts, Dublin, designed by James Gandon and built between 1786 and 1802.*

Left: *Daniel O'Connell (1775-1847), a political leader highly influential in the campaigns for Catholic emancipation and for the repeal of the Union.*

Right: *'Digging the Dinner' at Lifford in County Donegal, September 1894.*

Below: *a farmhouse in County Tyrone, 1899.*

The victory of 1829 facilitated a shift in the focus of political activity: parliament was now open to Catholic politics. During the 1830s O'Connell worked diligently in this different sphere, and through it he achieved notable changes for Ireland. Supporters of the tradition of physical force in Ireland have tended to be scathing about what can be achieved through compromise. Yet O'Connell's achievements – partial though they often tended to be – must surely be compared against the practical results which his physical force critics could offer. Hard line Irish republican movements have never been in particularly short supply of ambition. In terms of practical delivery of goods, their cupboard is slightly more bare. The exception to this is the phenomenon of physical force activism representing a strong hand in the background, a hand which can enable constitutional forces to exert greater pressure where it matters. Arguments could be made out along these lines with regard to Charles Parnell, or even to events concerning Northern Ireland in the 1980s. But such suggestions in no way damage the argument that constitutional methods of Irish political expression have enabled certain tangible results to be achieved.

Unfortunately for O'Connell, the latter years of his political career formed an anti-climactic end to his story. He sensed by 1840 that the Whig administration of Lord Melbourne would shortly be replaced by a less appealing Tory regime led by Robert Peel. O'Connell had publicly protested against the Union as early as 1800; now, in 1840, he founded the Repeal Association. This was to set the tone for important developments in the 1840s, and O'Connell returned to mass movement tactics in pursuit of repeal. The famous Clontarf episode of 1843 has become a lasting litmus test of attitudes to O'Connell; a repeal meeting planned for 8 October of that year was proscribed by the government and, rather than risk confrontation, O'Connell cancelled the gathering.

This raises the important question of O'Connell's hostile attitude toward political violence. O'Connell was firmly in the constitutionalist rather than the physical force camp. Right up until the present day there has been an ambiguity about the precise relationship between the violent and non-violent agendas in Irish nationalism. The former has largely been the preserve of an enthusiastic minority. Yet at certain crucial times the physical force approach has gained a wider measure of support (or at least of favourable acquiescence). To suggest that political violence in Ireland has always been the work of a few people with no connection to the wider public is to simplify a complex and important relationship. This extreme end of the political spectrum has tended to represent a concentrated and more narrowly conceived form of the wider nationalist rainbow.

O'Connell that Catholic Ireland emerged into political maturity, and he deserves to be recognised as one of Irish history's truly inspiring figures. Born in county Kerry, he was educated abroad and then became a barrister back home in Ireland. Talented and Catholic, he was in a perfect position to experience, respond to and do something about the injustices which Catholics suffered in the early nineteenth century. Debarred from sitting in parliament or holding high office, Catholics none the less had the potential within Ireland for the achievement of dominance. Focusing on the issue of Catholic emancipation, O'Connell helped Catholic Ireland to begin to realise this potential. In May 1823 he founded the Catholic Association, which sought the attainment of full political rights for Catholics. Charisma, oratory and organisational skills combined to make the man a formidable figure. And it was in the last of these spheres – that of organisation – that the crucial development occurred. The 'Catholic Rent' was a small subscription paid by thousands, and it offered both financial foundations and widespread political involvement. Thus mass politics arrived in Ireland and, significantly, the focus was a Catholic one. In 1828 O'Connell was elected MP for county Clare – as a Catholic he was unable to take his seat – and the following year saw the Catholic Emancipation Act, enabling Catholics to enter parliament and also to hold most public offices.

Left: *Merrion Square, Dublin. The second largest square in Dublin, this was completed at the end of the eighteenth century.*

Above: *St Finbarr's Cathedral, Cork. Situated on the River Lee, the city of Cork is Ireland's third largest and one of its most beautiful.*

During the 1840s something of this ambiguity came to life in the midst of the repeal agitation. In October 1842 the Nation was first published, a newspaper around which the Young Ireland movement developed. Young Ireland emerged within the context of O'Connell's repeal movement, but it was eventually to give birth to the next in the sequence of failed nationalist rebellions, that of 1848. The figures involved in Young Ireland included Thomas Davis (1814-45), Charles Gavan Duffy (1816-1903), John Blake Dillon (1816-66), John Mitchel (1815-75) and James Fintan Lalor (1807-49). Thus some of Irish nationalism's most famous names were associated with the Young Ireland movement. Of them all, Thomas Davis is perhaps the most attractive. A Protestant born in county Cork, he was educated at Dublin's Trinity College, became a lawyer, and between 1842 and 1845 effectively led the Young Ireland grouping. Like Wolfe Tone, Davis is an appealing and useful figure to cite if your creed is that of nationalism. As Protestants and anti-sectarians, these two men seem to some to provide a means of squaring an awkward circle. For nationalists face the problem in Ireland that the nationalist tradition early on became firmly fixed in the Catholic constituency. And it has been its Catholic identity which has done much to give it cohesion and meaning. In an attempt, however, to create a genuinely united Irish nation some separatists have maintained that true Irish nationalism involves non-denominational assumptions. The problem is clear. To maintain a Catholic ethos was to give nationalism an important identity; but this approach would result in the

Above: *the Fenian Banner. Launched in 1858, the Fenian movement aimed to achieve Irish independence from Britain by means of physical force.*

Left: *William Ewart Gladstone (1809-1898), the British Prime Minister who disestablished the Church of Ireland in 1869 and passed Irish land acts in 1870 and 1881.*

exclusion of a sizeable minority of the people from your nationalist world. To reject a Catholic ethos was to offer the hand of friendship to non-Catholics; but this approach would risk the loss of Catholic-generated momentum.

Thus Tone and Davis serve as useful icons. As Protestants they seem to deny the accusation that Irish nationalism is Catholic nationalism. They appear to present a model of nationalist Irishness which welcomes all creeds. The clash between unity and identity seems resolved. But this argument is deceptive, as events repeatedly proved. It is one thing to declare yourself opposed to sectarian division; it is quite another to achieve in practice the cross-sectarian unity that you desire. It was one thing to invite Ireland's Protestants to participate in the nationalist game; it was quite another – as Tone and Davis themselves found out – to establish a nationalist crusade in which significant numbers of Irish Protestants did in fact participate. Tone and Davis must be seen less as examples of any natural Protestant affinity with Irish separatism than as unrepresentative dissidents. That some (albeit charismatic) Protestants have joined the nationalist movement is less telling than the fact that the vast majority of Protestants have not done so.

Whatever the gulf between ideology and practice, Young Ireland left a major mark on Irish nationalist consciousness. Numerous of the people associated with the movement – such as the fiery Mitchel, or the agrarian radical Lalor – have become central figures within nationalist Irish history. And indeed the 1840s illuminate much about the development of Irish nationalism. There was, for example, considerable ambiguity about the precise nature of the objective which nationalists were pursuing. Roy Foster's assertion that, 'By "Repeal" O'Connell probably meant, first, a recognition of the illegitimacy of the Union; and then negotiation of an alternative mechanism of government' nicely reflects the blend which existed within the emerging nationalist tradition. This combination was to persist. Mitchel came to embody republicanism, while in comparison Davis showed signs of flexibility regarding federal arrangements. The historian Richard Davis has observed that, 'If there was considerable doubt

Right: Michael Davitt (1846-1906). Born in County Mayo, Davitt formed the Land League of Mayo and then the National Land League.

Below: Charles Stewart Parnell (1846-1891), first president of the Land League and leader of the Irish Parliamentary Party.

amongst Young Irelanders as to the ultimate ends of their movement, there was corresponding inconsistency on strategy'. As evidence of this he points to 'warlike exhilaration', 'passive constitutionalism' and 'insurrectionary aspirations'.

Yet such distinctions should not be overplayed. The fact that there was a variety of nationalist opinion should not lead us to dismiss the nationalist cause. The nineteenth century in Ireland witnessed the maturing of a political culture of autonomy. It should also be remembered that 'repeal' did offer a centre of gravity. As an aim it might have masked differences of outlook, but despite this it still represented a bonding ambition. The ambition was not achieved, however – it was to be the next century before the Union was fractured. Daniel O'Connell died in 1847, his career having fizzled rather unspectacularly in its latter stages. Thus the era of the mobiliser came to an end. O'Connell's demise occurred in Italy at a time when Ireland was experiencing famine. Famine was in fact no newcomer to Ireland, but the horrors of the late 1840s were exceptional. Understandably tattooed on the memory of the island, the trauma emerged as a result of a fungal disease which struck the potato in Ireland. The potato having become a staple food by the 1840s, its infection wrought atrocious results. Despite the speedy relief inaugurated by prime minister Robert Peel, massive

Left: *Belfast City Hall, a Renaissance palazzo designed by Sir Brumwell Thomas and built between 1898 and 1906.*

Right: *Church of Ireland St Anne's Cathedral, Belfast, which contains the tomb of Edward Carson.*

Below: *Queen's University, Belfast, established in 1849 and incorporated as a university in its own right in 1908.*

Above: *Cork market in the 1890s.*

tragedy hit the island. Disease, starvation, exposure and emigration between them decimated the Irish population. Between 1845 and 1851, it has been estimated, over two million inhabitants died or emigrated. This remains a staggering haemorrhage.

The authorities' behaviour contributed to the extent of the suffering. Lord John Russell (prime minister between 1846 and 1852) adhered to *laissez-faire* economic thinking, with the result that state intervention was limited. The idea was that local rather than central initiative should primarily be relied on to deal with the situation. Though fashionable, this notion was deeply unrealistic. Accusations that the British engaged in the partial genocide of the Irish are historically daft. But it remains the case that the government was hopelessly inept at dealing with conditions in famine Ireland. The impact of the tragedy, of course, was far from evenly distributed. Regional and class-based differences of experience were enormous. The east of Leinster and the northeast of Ulster escaped

comparatively unscathed, for example. In terms of class it was labourers and smaller farmers who suffered most heavily. Yet distinctions such as these have often been obscured in more generalised reactions to the period.

One important nineteenth century trend to which the famine significantly contributed was that of emigration. The scale of this was such that 'Irishness' became less reliant upon the island itself. The growth of Irish communities in Britain, Canada, Australia and – above all – the United States added a new layer to the complexity of Irish experience. The problem for Irish nationalism in Ireland was that significant numbers of people there rejected the emerging nationalist tradition. Yet outside Ireland there existed many people with a sturdy commitment to this same tradition. The mobilisation of this non-resident sentiment was one aspiration of the Fenian movement. This secret society was launched on St Patrick's day, 1858, in Dublin by James Stephens (1825-1901). Mystery was to be an important element within the

Above: *Harland and Wolff workers leaving their shift in April 1914. This Belfast shipyard has played a vital part in the city's economic history.*

Right: *a late-nineteenth-century eviction scene. The threat of eviction was very real for many tenants.*

Overleaf: *Upper Lake Killarney, County Kerry.*

Irish independence tended to eclipse all other concerns. And while not every leading Fenian was a traditional republican, there was a distinctly republican flavour to this conspiratorial tradition. Indeed, it seems that the initial Fenian oath – which originated with Thomas Clarke Luby – included a commitment to create an Irish republic.

The Fenians aimed to achieve independence by force. Dallying with constitutionalism was held to be a fruitless pastime. They argued that English conversion to the idea of Irish independence could only come as a result of the use of violence. There emerged a firmly committed physical force approach; where the 1790s or 1840s had produced rebellion after other methods had failed, the Fenians embarked from the start on the road to bloodshed. Yet there were similarities between Fenian violence and that of earlier rebellions. The nineteenth century Fenians failed in practical terms, just as the attempted insurrections of 1798, 1803 or 1848 had, and the Fenian rising of 1867 was comfortably crushed by the authorities.

A further similarity which the Fenians shared with earlier Irish revolutionaries was that their military gestures subsequently came to achieve celebrity status in the republican tradition of the twentieth century. Thus 1867 joined the other magic numbers – 1798, 1803 and so on – in an ever-expanding

Fenian tradition and even the organisation's name was initially hard to locate. The Irish Republican Brotherhood (IRB); the Irish Revolutionary Brotherhood; the Fenian Brotherhood; the Fenians; more menacingly, perhaps, the 'organisation' – each of these terms has been used in connection with the same grouping. Its concentration on the objective of

collection of historic dates. One other point about the Fenians which is worth consideration is their social composition. Writing to Engels in November 1867, Karl Marx claimed that, 'Fenianism is characterised by a socialistic tendency (in a negative sense, directed against the appropriation of the soil) and by being a lower orders movement'. There were better grounds for the latter than for the former of these claims. It is interesting also to note Marx's comments on the Fenian attempt on 13 December 1867 to rescue one of their number from London's Clerkenwell prison; the explosion which formed part of the rescue bid caused numerous deaths and injuries. In a letter written the following day to Engels, Marx commented that:

The last exploit of the Fenians in Clerkenwell was a very stupid thing. The London masses, who have shown great sympathy for Ireland, will be made wild by it and driven into the arms of the government party. One cannot expect the London proletarians to allow themselves to be blown up in honour of the Fenian emissaries.

Sound sense indeed. And yet prisoners have played a vital part within the Irish republican tradition. More successful propaganda than the Clerkenwell explosion could and did emerge from the phenomenon of republican incarceration.

At this stage we should perhaps move on to look at one of Irish history's most influential figures: Charles Stewart Parnell (1846-91). Parnell's career was to be influenced by his relations with the physical force tradition. Born in county Wicklow, Parnell had an Anglo-Irish, land-owning father and an American mother with Ulster Presbyterian roots. He went to Cambridge University and was in 1875 elected to parliament as a Home Rule MP. In 1870 the Home Government Association had been founded by Isaac Butt (1813-79), with a view to the achievement of an Irish parliament. In 1873 the Association matured into the Home Rule League. The election of 1874 saw the emergence in the London parliament of a Home Rule party led by Butt, and it was in this parliamentary context that Parnell began his political innings.

To Isaac Butt, home government meant the establishment (or re-establishment) of a domestic Irish parliament which would exist within an imperial framework. Thus it was not total separation from Britain that was being espoused; rather the call was for a form of legislative autonomy for Ireland. The Home Rule movement which grew from Butt's beginnings was to become very much Parnell's crusade. In 1877 Parnell became president of the Home Rule Confederation of Great Britain. In 1880 he became chairman of the Irish Parliamentary Party. But Parnell's political importance was associated

with the breadth of his vision and practice. Not only did he lead the charge towards Home Rule, but he also threw out seductive hints in the direction of those who might seek a fuller degree of independence for Ireland. Thus, in January 1885 Parnell declared:

We cannot ask for less than the restitution of Grattan's parliament …. We cannot under the British constitution ask for more than the restitution of Grattan's parliament, but no man has the right to fix the boundary to the march of a nation. No man has a right to say to his country, "Thus far shalt thou go and no further", and we have never attempted to fix the ne plus ultra to the progress of Ireland's nationhood, and we never shall.

Grattan's parliament represented Irish legislative independence within a British framework. Yet here Parnell was being deliberately unclear about Irish national ambitions. Was Grattan's parliament a satisfactory goal? Were things meant to go on beyond the attainment of legislative independence under the crown?

Ambiguity of a different kind can be detected in the late-nineteenth-century relation between land issues and the national question. In 1879 the Irish National Land League had been founded, with Parnell becoming its president. The League's stated aims were:

First, to bring about a reduction of rack-rents; second, to facilitate the obtaining of the ownership of the soil by the occupiers.

The 1870s and 1880s in Ireland were heavily coloured by the questions of Home Rule and land politics. And Parnell was now crucial in both realms. The precise relation between land and national politics in this period is a complex one. Michael Davitt's influential role in the politics of the land is interesting here, given his Fenian credentials. And Parnell's own rhetoric could hint at a practical relationship between the land and national movements in this period. At Galway in October 1880 he argued that, while wishing to see Irish tenant farmers prosper, he would not have dived into the land agitation 'if I had not known that we were laying the foundations by

this movement for the recovery of our legislative independence'.

Thus Parnell wove a web of political alliances which – for a time, at least – held diverse forces in a seemingly implausible pattern. A parliamentarian, he won admiration from devotees of violence. Successful in the attainment of Catholic church support for Home Rule, he also threw out lines towards the physical force tradition against which the church had firmly set its face. Parliamentary party, tenant farmers, Catholic church, physical force people – and even for a time the London government – each of these powerful ingredients was involved in the politics of Parnell. Thus in 1886 William Ewart Gladstone (1809-98) introduced the first Home Rule Bill, which would have established an Irish parliament within an imperial context. In the mid 1880s Parnell found himself holding the balance of power at Westminster. Gladstone could only assume office should Parnell give him his backing. This Parnell did; Gladstone became prime minister and the relationship between the two men and between their respective parties was cemented.

Below: *an Ulster Unionist convention held in Belfast's Botanic Gardens in 1892.*

Right: *Unionist leader Edward Carson acknowledging the cheers of Ulster Volunteers in 1914.*

Below: *12 July parade commemorating the Battle of the Boyne, in Dublin Road, Belfast, in 1901.*

Left: *the Sackville Street area of Dublin during the Easter Rising of 1916.*

Right: *the General Post Office, O'Connell Street, Dublin, from which the 1916 rebel proclamation was issued.*

Below left: *British troops behind a street barricade during the 1916 Rising.*

Below: *Henry Street, damaged by shells in April 1916. The rebellion was crushed by the authorities within a week.*

The first Home Rule Bill was in fact defeated in the House of Commons by 343 votes to 313. The later Home Rule Bills (of 1893 and 1912) also met unpleasant ends – though the Home Rule idea was eventually to triumph. Gladstone's 1893 measure was defeated in the House of Lords. The Bill which emerged in 1912 reached the statute book in 1914; but it was decided that its operation should be suspended until after the end of the First World War. By the time that the war did in fact end, in 1918, circumstances had greatly changed. Parnell's political and then actual demise only partially, therefore, marked a break in Irish history. One of Ireland's most sophisticated and influential political leaders was gone, and it was natural that a kind of vacuum should ensue. But much continued after 1891 of the world which Parnell had helped to mould. As noted, the concept of Home Rule persisted. Above all, perhaps, the land revolution was fundamental to the development of the modern Ireland. In 1870 Gladstone's first Land Act had recognised certain principles of tenant protection and, although in practice little change was effected, this measure proved to be a sign of the direction of the coming tides. In 1881 a further Land Act provided for a land court which would fix rents fairly, decreed that those who paid such rents should be guaranteed against eviction, and made a further gesture regarding a tenant's right of free sale. In 1885 the Ashbourne Act made moves in the direction of land purchase. In 1891 a further step was taken along this path, while in 1903 the Wyndham Act located land purchase as the answer to Ireland's land question.

So it was that peasant proprietorship set the tone for modern Irish rural society. And the other two subversive forces of significance, unionism and nationalism, undoubtedly involve much complexity. Thus the logic of past interests crystallised in the form of Catholic, Gaelic nationalism and Protestant, non-Gaelic unionism. Plainly, not everybody fell neatly into this scheme. But the lines of division were clear enough. Unionist opposition to Home Rule was fierce and massive, as was reflected in the signing of the Solemn League and Covenant in 1912:

Being convinced in our consciences that Home Rule would be disastrous to the material well-being of Ulster as well as the whole of Ireland, subversive of our civil and religious freedom, destructive of our citizenship, and perilous to the unity of the Empire [we] do hereby pledge ourselves … to stand by one another in defending for ourselves and our children our cherished position of equal citizenship in the United Kingdom and in using all means which may be found necessary to defeat the present conspiracy to set up a Home Rule Parliament.

Left: *Patrick Pearse (1879-1916), the charismatic leader of the April 1916 rebellion, executed in May 1916: 'We have the strength and the peace of mind of those who never compromise.'*

Facing page top left: *James Connolly (1868-1916), a labour leader and a major figure in the 1916 Rising.*

Below: *Constance Markievicz (1868-1927), who, as a Sinn Fein representative, became the first woman to be elected to the House of Commons.*

Below: *Pearse cottage, Connemara, County Galway, where Patrick Pearse wrote much of his poetry. The nationalist leader did much to promote the Irish language.*

Right: *signatories to the Declaration of the Republic, 1916.*

Below: *Eamon de Valera (1882-1975), founder of the Fianna Fáil Party, three-time prime minister of Ireland, and symbol of an independent nation.*

THOMAS J. CLARKE—*1857-1916*

First Signatory of the Proclamation of the Irish Republic —Easter, 1916.

Sentenced to penal servitude for life on 14th June, 1883. Released in 1898 after serving 15 years.

He was executed at Kilmainham on May 3rd, 1916 and buried at Arbour Hill.

PÁDRAIG PEARSE—*1879-1916*

Born Dublin 10th November, 1879.

Educated Christian Brothers School, Westland Row, Dublin and University College, Dublin.

Called to the Bar 1901.

Appointed editor of " An Claidheamh Solais" 1903.

Founded Scoil Éanna, 1908.

A Signatory of the Proclamation of the Irish Republic —Easter, 1916.

Commander-in-Chief of the Forces of the Irish Republic.

Executed at Kilmainham Prison on May 3rd, 1916, and buried at Arbour Hill Military Prison.

JAMES CONNOLLY, *1870-1916*

Born near Clones, Co. Monaghan, 1870.

Founded Irish Socialist Federation, U.S.A., 1908.

Founded " The Harp " in U.S.A., 1908.

Member of the I.R.B. Military Council, 1915.

Officer Commanding the Citizen Army.

Commandant General of the Dublin Area Easter, 1916.

A Signatory of the Proclamation of the Republic, Easter, 1916.

Executed at Kilmainham Prison on 12th May, 1916, and buried at Arbour Hill Military Prison.

SEÁN MAC DIARMADA, *1884-1916*

Born Glenfarac, Co. Leitrim, 1884.

Joined I.R.B. in Belfast, 1903.

Organiser Sinn Féin, 1906-1909.

Publisher of " Irish Freedom," 1909-1914.

A Signatory of the Proclamation of the Irish Republic —Easter, 1916.

Executed at Kilmainham Prison on May 12th, 1916, and buried at Arbour Hill Military Prison.

EAMONN CEANNT, *1881-1916*

Born in Co. Galway, 1881.

Educated at O'Connell Schools, North Richmond Street, Dublin.

Member of the Coiste Gnótha of the Gaelic League.

Member of the National Council of Sinn Féin.

Member of the Executive of the Irish Volunteers.

Member of the Military Council which planned the Insurrection of 1916.

A Signatory of the Proclamation of the Republic, Easter 1916.

Commanded the Fourth Battalion of the Irish Volunteers which garrisoned the South Dublin Union and the post in Marrowbone Lane.

Tried by British Field General Court Martial and sentenced to death.

Executed at Kilmainham Prison on the 8th May, 1916, and buried at Arbour Hill Military Prison.

JOSEPH PLUNKETT, *1887-1916*

Born in Dublin 1887.

Eldest son of George Noble Count Plunkett.

Educated at Belvedere College, Dublin and Stonyhurst, England.

Poet and writer.

Member of Provisional Committee of the Irish Volunteers, 1913-14.

Member of the Irish Volunteer Executive, 1914-16.

Member of the Headquarters Staff, Irish Volunteers, 1915-16.

Member of the Military Council, Irish Republican Brotherhood, 1915-16.

A Signatory of the Proclamation of the Republic, Easter Week, 1916.

Tried by British Field General Court Martial, sentenced to death, and executed at Kilmainham Prison on the 4th May, 1916.

Buried at Arbour Hill Military Prison, Dublin.

POBLACHT NA H EIREANN.
THE PROVISIONAL GOVERNMENT
OF THE
IRISH REPUBLIC
TO THE PEOPLE OF IRELAND.

IRISHMEN AND IRISHWOMEN: In the name of God and of the dead generations from which she receives her old tradition of nationhood, Ireland, through us, summons her children to her flag and strikes for her freedom.

Having organised and trained her manhood through her secret revolutionary organisation, the Irish Republican Brotherhood, and through her open military organisations, the Irish Volunteers and the Irish Citizen Army, having patiently perfected her discipline, having resolutely waited for the right moment to reveal itself, she now seizes that moment, and, supported by her exiled children in America and by gallant allies in Europe, but relying in the first on her own strength, she strikes in full confidence of victory.

We declare the right of the people of Ireland to the ownership of Ireland, and to the unfettered control of Irish destinies, to be sovereign and indefeasible. The long usurpation of that right by a foreign people and government has not extinguished the right, nor can it ever be extinguished except by the destruction of the Irish people. In every generation the Irish people have asserted their right to national freedom and sovereignty; six times during the past three hundred years they have asserted it in arms. Standing on that fundamental right and again asserting it in arms in the face of the world, we hereby proclaim the Irish Republic as a Sovereign Independent State, and we pledge our lives and the lives of our comrades-in-arms to the cause of its freedom, of its welfare, and of its exaltation among the nations.

The Irish Republic is entitled to, and hereby claims, the allegiance of every Irishman and Irishwoman. The Republic guarantees religious and civil liberty, equal rights and equal opportunities to all its citizens, and declares its resolve to pursue the happiness and prosperity of the whole nation and of all its parts, cherishing all the children of the nation equally, and oblivious of the differences carefully fostered by an alien government, which have divided a minority from the majority in the past.

Until our arms have brought the opportune moment for the establishment of a permanent National Government, representative of the whole people of Ireland and elected by the suffrages of all her men and women, the Provisional Government, hereby constituted, will administer the civil and military affairs of the Republic in trust for the people.

We place the cause of the Irish Republic under the protection of the Most High God, Whose blessing we invoke upon our arms, and we pray that no one who serves that cause will dishonour it by cowardice, inhumanity, or rapine. In this supreme hour the Irish nation must, by its valour and discipline and by the readiness of its children to sacrifice themselves for the common good, prove itself worthy of the august destiny to which it is called.

Signed on Behalf of the Provisional Government,
THOMAS J. CLARKE,
SEAN Mac DIARMADA, THOMAS MacDONAGH,
P. H. PEARSE, EAMONN CEANNT,
JAMES CONNOLLY, JOSEPH PLUNKETT.

THOMAS MacDONAGH, *1878-1916*

Born Cloughjordan, Co. Tipperary, 1878.

Educated Rockwell College and National University of Ireland.

Founder-Member of the Irish Theatre, Hardwicke Street, Dublin, 1914.

Poet and Author of distinction.

Adjutant, Dublin Brigade Irish Volunteers, 1916.

Member of Military Council of the I.R.B., 1916.

A Signatory of the Proclamation of the Republic, Easter, 1916.

Executed at Kilmainham Prison on the 3rd May, 1916, and buried at Arbour Hill Military Prison.

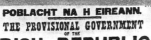

Right: Eamon de Valera (left), the single most important figure in the political history of modern Ireland.

Left: Richard Mulcahy (marked with a cross), Commander in Chief of the Irish Army, addressing the Dail in the early 1920s.

Below left: British troops at the entrance to the pier at Dun Laoghaire awaiting the arrival of de Valera in 1919.

Below: the Irish Declaration of Independence was drawn up in Dublin's Mansion House by the Dail Eireann in January of 1919. Here, members of the militant Irish Volunteers – later known as the Irish Republican Army – stand on duty nearby during the sitting of the Dail.

In a sense Pearse's career followed the logic of the nationalist condition. The Gaelic Athletic Association would aim to guard and develop native Irish sports; the Gaelic League would seek to promote the Irish language. These were cultural attempts to fight against the Anglicisation of Ireland. But these were mirrored by a political struggle, to free Ireland from English control in that realm also. Pearse was a feverishly dedicated Gaelic Leaguer, and in 1913 he was a founder member of the Irish Volunteers. He also joined the Irish Republican Brotherhood (IRB) and indeed it was as a revolutionary that he was to attain later celebrity status. Pearse's fame rests primarily on the 1916 rebellion – though over-concentration on this part of his career has tended to obscure the importance of his earlier enthusiasms. The Easter 1916 insurrection ostensibly aimed to establish an independent Irish republic. In reality its significance lies in its quality of military gesture. By the time that the rebellion actually began (on 24 April 1916), it had little realistic chance of success. But the proclamation which Pearse read out in Dublin on that opening day of the revolt became one of the sacred texts of the Irish republican tradition:

We declare the right of the people of Ireland to the ownership of Ireland, and to the unfettered control of Irish destinies, to be sovereign and indefeasible. The long usurpation of that right by a foreign people and government has not extinguished the right, nor can it ever be extinguished except by the destruction of the Irish people .... The Irish republic is entitled to, and hereby claims, the allegiance of every Irishman and Irishwoman. The republic guarantees religious and civil liberty, equal rights and equal opportunities to all its citizens, and declares its resolve to pursue the happiness and prosperity of the whole nation and of all its parts, cherishing all the children of the nation equally, and oblivious of the differences carefully fostered by an alien government, which have divided a minority from the majority in the past .... In this supreme hour the Irish nation must, by its valour and discipline, and by the readiness of its children to sacrifice themselves for the common good, prove itself worthy of the august destiny to which it is called.

Signed on behalf of the provisional government, Thomas J. Clarke, Sean MacDiarmada, Thomas MacDonagh, P.H. Pearse, Eamonn Ceannt, James Connolly, Joseph Plunkett.

The perception of threat is illuminated here by the words, 'disastrous', 'subversive', 'destructive', 'perilous' and 'conspiracy'. The following year the Ulster Volunteer Force (UVF) was established. Plans were drawn up for a provisional government, and by the time firearms and ammunition were landed in 1914, the basis for a sturdy bout of resistance had unquestionably been laid.

Cultural and paramilitary resistance was also emerging from another quarter. The Irish Volunteers were established in November 1913 to provide a nationalist counter-gesture. It was fitting that the genesis of the Irish Volunteers should owe so much to Eoin MacNeill, since he reflected the trend towards cultural Irish nationalism which was so important at the turn of the century. In 1884 the Gaelic Athletic Association had been set up. And in 1893 the Gaelic League had been established, with Douglas Hyde as its first president and with MacNeill as its first vice-president. The emphasis on Gaelic culture was to have vast influence in twentieth century Irish nationalism. The most significant icon in modern Irish republicanism was Patrick Pearse (1879-1916). Born in Dublin, Pearse was called to the Bar ,but chose instead a kind of alternative professionalism expressed through cultural, educational, and in the end revolutionary, enthusiasm.

The reference to sacrifice is important. The rebels were defeated in 1916, surrendering on 29 April. Pearse was executed on 3 May, and thereby won the right to the status of nationalist martyr. As we have seen, the cult of the dying hero had roots in earlier Irish history; Pearse himself, incidentally, made much of Theobald Wolfe Tone. As one of the most charismatic of twentieth century republicans – Ernie O'Malley (1897-1957) – put it: 'As a Republican one was evidently never sufficiently tested until one had died in the Republican faith'. The republican faith was propelled forward, ironically, by Britain's involvement in the First World War. Not only did the war seem to some to offer an opportunity of striking at a distracted England, but the threatened imposition of conscription on Ireland served powerfully to alienate many people from the authorities.

A combination of factors therefore united to stimulate nationalist Ireland into a new stage of activity – the suppression of the 1916 rising, the reorganisation of the Sinn Fein movement in 1917, the tactless handling by the British of the conscription issue. But even at the point of Sinn Fein's apparent triumph – when it thrashed the Irish Parliamentary Party in the 1918 general election – the picture was far less neat than might initially have been assumed. For one thing the election also demonstrated the strength of unionist opposition to nationalist aspirations. The twenty-six unionists elected in 1918 were greatly outnumbered, it is true, by the seventy-three Sinn Feiners. But the geographical concentration of unionist commitment in Ireland was destined to present problems for Irish nationalists. If nationalist Ireland derived strength and cohesion from its Gaelic, Catholic identity, then what did this imply about the 'Irishness' of non-Gaelic non-Catholics who lived on the island? And what use was it anyway to invite unionists into your proposed all-Ireland nation if they firmly rejected your offer; would you – could you – force them to accept your invitation?

Such problems were to cause lasting and painful headaches for Irish nationalists. The tradition which produced nationalist leaders such as Arthur Griffith (1871-1922) and Eamon de Valera (1882-1975) was matched in commitment, though not in numbers, by that which produced unionist figures such as Edward Carson (1854-1935) and James Craig (1871-1940). But in the immediate post-war period the tide seemed to flow with the nationalist cause. The Anglo-Irish war began in 1919 and was to continue until 1921. An ambush in county Tipperary can be interpreted as inaugurating the military conflict – though it took some time for momentum to develop. On the same day, 21 January 1919, in Dublin took place the first meeting of an alternative Irish parliament – *Dail Eireann*. The membership of the Dail was composed of people who had been elected in the general election of 1918. Thus it was out of the womb of the United Kingdom's electoral process that the independently-minded Irish nationalist child emerged.

Left: Charles Villiers Stanford (1852-1924), a Dublin-born composer.

Facing page top left: Lady Gregory (1852-1932), director of the Abbey Theatre Company and writer of over forty plays.

Below: the Dublin-born writer Oscar Wilde (1854-1900).

Right: *the Irish-born tenor John McCormack (1884-1945).*

Below: *a copy of an original theatre bill for the Abbey Theatre in 1916.*

CHAPTER FIVE

THE MODERN ISLAND

IRELAND SINCE 1920

And anything that happened to me afterwards,
I never felt the same about again.

FRANK O'CONNOR

The sun shone, having no alternative, on the
nothing new.

SAMUEL BECKETT

Ambiguity surrounds the Anglo-Irish war. The exact relationship between the military and non-military forces for independence; the precise interpretation which nationalists gave to their objective; the question of whether what eventually emerged from the conflict would have emerged anyway without it – these and other areas remain open to a considerable measure of debate. What can safely be asserted is that a multi-pronged independence movement succeeded by 1921 in prodding the British government into the granting of partial Irish independence. The Anglo-Irish war was ended with a truce in July 1921. Negotiations between British and Irish representatives resulted in the fiercely disputed 'treaty' of December 1921. This arrangement offered substantial rather than total independence for twenty-six of Ireland's thirty-two counties.

The six northeastern counties excluded from the new state were Antrim, Londonderry, Tyrone, Fermanagh, Armagh and Down. But partition had effectively existed prior to the signing of the 1921 treaty. The Government of Ireland Act of 1920 provided for the setting up of a northern and of a southern parliament – each enjoying powers of local self-government – and the former was in fact opened by king George V in June 1921. The Government of Ireland Act southern parliament had not become a reality, but when *Dail Eireann* approved the treaty in January 1922 the process of partition became more

firmly established. For the setting up of the Irish Free State under the terms of the 1921 treaty carved a territorial division in Ireland which has ever since persisted. In part this merely recognised realities. A sizeable concentration of people in the northeast of the island wanted nothing to do with Irish independence, and so remained attached to Britain. Yet the split between north and south was anything but neat. The historic province of Ulster contained nine counties, not six, and many Protestant people were cut adrift by partition and left in counties Donegal, Monaghan and Cavan. There was also in Northern Ireland a large minority of Catholic people who now faced life on the 'wrong' side of the border. The truth was that the six-county state was decided upon since it was held to provide the largest area over which a unionist regime could securely preside.

Partition also served to further the likelihood of self-deceptions regarding identity. One vital theme in Irish history has been the persistence of the desire for dominance and the failure adequately to attain it. Something of this was to become painfully apparent within the context of partitioned Ireland. There developed in Northern Ireland a conviction that 'Ulster was British' – a conviction which failed to admit the existence within the six counties of a significant number of nationalists. But in the southern state Irishness continued to be portrayed in terms which alienated many on the island.

Above: *Michael Collins (1890-1922) – born in County Cork, was the outstanding military figure on the Irish side of the War of Independence.*

Below: *members of the RIC, apparently in good humour, in 1920.*

Right: *British troops in Dublin, during the 1919-1920 Anglo-Irish war.*

Below: *members of the security forces, apparently in good humour, in 1920.*

Partition was not, however, the main topic of debate during the Dail's discussion of the proposed treaty. While the 1921 Anglo-Irish agreement had offered substantial autonomy to the intended southern state, it was none the less objectionable to many within the independence movement. The narrowness of the vote in the Dail in January 1922 – sixty-four in favour of the treaty, fifty-seven against – pointed to some of the difficulties which lay ahead. But it also suggested a willingness to give the treaty a chance. In a sense the nationalist achievement of the Anglo-Irish war had been one of propaganda and of personality. Violence was impressively portrayed in terms of victories and of atrocities. The Irish Republican Army (IRA) which grew out of the Irish Volunteers was celebrated in heroic terms. To quote again from the eminent IRA man, Ernie O'Malley: 'I was told stories of myself, what I had said or done in different places. I could not recognize myself for the legend.' In contrast, the actions of the forces of the crown – some of which were indeed

atrocious – became celebrated in a negative sense. The establishment of the Dail – an alternative Irish government – symbolised the maturity of nationalist Ireland. Was not here a governmental culture in waiting? Was it not obvious that legitimacy rested with this body elected by Irish people?

But the civil war which occurred in 1922-3 shone a spotlight on the tensions which had existed within the independence movement. Personality might have seemed to pioneer the way to freedom up to 1921. But in the post-treaty split the gods were shown warring amongst themselves. Michael Collins (1890-1922) – who, perhaps, did more than anyone else to achieve the successful draw of 1921 – was important in pushing through the treaty. Arthur Griffith – with Collins, a co-signatory of the 1921 agreement – was another influential pro-treatyite. Yet to their anti-treaty opponents these figures had betrayed the republic, had settled for less than was Ireland's right and had cooperated in a disgraceful compromise. The fact that the treaty offered complete independence

Left: *Muckross House, County Kerry, built in 1843 and now housing a folk museum.*

Below: *children in a Dublin street, waving American flags and celebrating the end of the Anglo-Irish war in 1921.*

in domestic matters did not count for anything – so the argument ran – for the Irish Free State was not the Irish republic. Michael Collins argued that

> *After a national struggle sustained through many centuries, we have to-day in Ireland a native Government deriving its authority solely from the Irish people, and acknowledged by England and the other nations of the world.*

But neither this, nor the assertion that the 'substance of freedom' had been attained, could convince anti-treaty opponents. The anti-treaty republicans opposed the idea of the oath with passionate hostility. Under the terms of the 1921 treaty, members of the Free State parliament were obliged to take an oath of allegiance to the British monarch. The ferocity of response which this provoked indicated the quality of opposition to the agreement. Just as a republic had been fought for, so the British crown was what had been fought against. The republic embodied all that was desired; the crown represented all that was detested. To fight for the former and end up owing allegiance to the latter was unthinkable to many in 1922.

In April 1922 anti-treaty republicans took over Dublin's Four Courts building and set up headquarters there. On 28 June the Four Courts was attacked by the forces of the pro-treaty government. Two days later the republican garrison surrendered. This battle of the Four Courts marked the beginning of the Irish civil war. The war lasted until the following year. In 1923 Eamon de Valera – the anti-treaty leader – issued a proclamation addressed to the republican army:

> *Further sacrifice on your part would now be vain and continuance of the struggle in arms unwise in the national interest. Military victory must be allowed to rest for the moment with those who have destroyed the Republic.*

The IRA chief of staff, Frank Aiken, issued an order for republican forces to cease fire and dump their weapons. The civil war was officially over. The Free State – which had come into formal existence in December 1922 – had won the day. But the election of August 1923 reflected the fact that deep divisions remained within the infant state. In March 1923 the pro-treaty party, Cumann na nGaedheal, had been launched, and in the August election this grouping won 63 seats in a Dail of 153. The republicans won 44 Dail seats, and though their policy of parliamentary abstention rendered this less dramatic, it was none the less an indication of resilient support. The republic may have been betrayed in the treaty and defeated in the battlefield of the civil war, but the republican tradition still breathed.

William Cosgrave (1880-1965) led the Cumann na nGaedheal government which ruled the Free State between 1922 and 1932. Far less charismatic than many contemporary figures in political Ireland, he presided over a swiftly maturing state. At first glance the emergence of a stable Free State out of the

Right: *"B" Specials, who were part of the Ulster Special Constabulary, on duty at a bank in Strabane in 1922.*

Below: *IRA volunteers on the march in 1922.*

dislocation of two wars seems striking. Having experienced a conflict with a powerful external enemy between 1919 and 1921, Ireland then witnessed a vicious contest between internal political groupings between 1922 and 1923. The civil war as much reflected as created the tensions of the territory. Its legacy of bitterness has often been noted. That this legacy developed is hardly surprising. Incarceration, assassination, execution and hunger strike encouraged acrimonious memory. On 7 December 1922, pro-treaty Dail member Sean Hales was killed by republicans. The government speedily responded; on 8 December 1922 four republican prisoners (Liam Mellows, Rory O'Connor, Joe McKelvey and Dick Barrett) were executed in Dublin's Mountjoy Jail. Fellow republican prisoner Peadar O'Donnell (1893-1986) wrote with reference to the 8 December executions:

I got the news in the door of the chapel. I just went wooden. I was completely dried of all feeling. I saw men sob and I heard men curse but the whole chapel was detached …. The wing that day was a grave; we were a wordless, soulless movement of lives suddenly empty.

The republican hunger strike for unconditional release, occurring in October/November 1923, served both to reflect the strength of commitment of the post-civil war republicans and also to point to their weakness. The strike was called off in November 1923 without any promise of release having been wrested from the Free State authorities. Defeated in the Dail over the treaty, defeated militarily in the civil war, the republic was now beaten, too, in the post-war prisons.

And this should not surprise us. For all its seductive rhetoric and commitment, the Irish republicanism of the revolutionary period was destined for defeat. Its aspirations for the total independence of the thirty-two counties implied the inevitability of disappointment. British and Ulster resistance to the idea of an Irish republic was too high a fence for revolutionary separatists to clear. They could generate the conditions within which important concessions would be granted. But they had not the power with which to force their ambitions to completion. Part of the 1919-21 nationalist experience was the adoption of strong poses regarding the aims that were sought. But commitment to the poses greatly varied. So, for some a thirty-two county 'republic' was the least they would accept. Yet others, plainly, were ready quite swiftly to climb down from the high ground of republican hope to the less lofty level of the Irish Free State. Compromise, indeed, was implicit in any serious approach to negotiation; thus the 1921 Anglo-Irish negotiations might seem to have implied some willingness to compromise. And compromise was, in practice, inevitable given the respective strengths and commitments involved. But to intransigent republicans there could be no backing down. In arguing that the 1921 treaty represented 'the betrayal of the Republic', Liam Mellows embodied this tradition; 'I stand now where I always stood, for the Irish Republic ... I hold you cannot deny the existence of the Irish Republic and remain a Republican. This Treaty is a denial of the Republic.'

Mellows was a mystical soldier of the republic, a crusader on behalf of Irish independence. But the crusade lacked the power to overcome the obstacles in the way of its full success. Offered a substantial measure of freedom in 1921, a majority chose compromise. The diehard republicans could only succeed when their concerns were shared by large numbers of the people. This was the case in 1920; it was no longer so in 1923. Ironically, perhaps, the person who did most to marginalise the hard core republican tradition in the southern state was Eamon de Valera. De Valera came to recognise the necessity for compromise. In 1926 he formed a new political party, Fianna Fail, which was to come to dominate southern political life. In 1927 for the first time Fianna Fail entered the twenty-six county Dail. They thus balanced the previously lop-sided, Cumann na nGaedheal-dominated institution. In 1932 Fianna Fail came to power, having mobilised much support among the old anti-treaty constituency. During the 1930s de Valera's party set about the removal of numerous elements of the treaty arrangement. The land annuities payments to Britain, the oath of allegiance to the British crown, the office of governor-general, the senate – each of these features of the treaty state was abolished.

In 1937 de Valera's new constitution set the philosophy of his Ireland. It named the state, 'Eire, or in the English language, Ireland'. It also recognised realities in its attitude to Northern Ireland. The national territory was defined as including all thirty-two counties. Thus the heritage and identity of Irish nationalist aspiration were respectfully enshrined in the sacred text of de Valera's Ireland. But the inability of nationalist Ireland to achieve the united independence of the island was also recognised. For the constitution declared that, pending the restoration of the six counties, the jurisdiction of the Dublin government would extend only over the twenty-six county area. This approach epitomised the contradictions of Irish nationalism. The constitution asserted an all-Ireland case; yet it simultaneously embodied certain attitudes guaranteed to provoke hostility among Ulster unionists. The 'special position' of the Catholic church (acknowledged in this 1937 document) was hardly likely to win many Protestant friends in counties Down or Antrim!

But two other points should perhaps be given greater stress. First, the nationalist tradition had for years derived strength from its Catholic, Gaelic emphases. The fact that these had tended to exclude non-Gaelic non-Catholics had not in fact eroded their importance in giving momentum to the

Right: *the Four Courts, Dublin. In June 1922, government forces attacked the republicans who were occupying the Four Courts.*

Below: *the battle of the Four Courts, Dublin, 1922; this is held as marking the start of the Irish civil war.*

nationalist march. Indeed, it was extremely convenient that the northeastern counties were partitioned. Second, it should also be noted that Ulster unionist hostility to Irish unity was sturdy enough regardless of the 1937 constitution. There was little sign that unionists were willing to move toward unity in any circumstances anyway.

If his *constitution* was a crucial document, de Valera's *party* held a dominant position in the life of the southern state. This was reflected in the fact that Fianna Fail were in office for two impressive sixteen-year stretches (1932-48 and 1957-73) and it was during the first of these periods that Ireland underwent her distinctive Second World War experiences. In September 1939 the southern state adopted a neutral stance. This was a position it maintained throughout the conflict, though not without certain tensions developing at times with belligerent nations.

Three years after the end of the war Fianna Fail fell from power. Between 1948 and 1951 the state was governed by a coalition led by John A. Costello as Taoiseach (or prime minister). Costello's party – Fine Gael – had emerged from the Cumann na

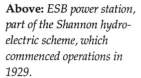
Above: *ESB power station, part of the Shannon hydro-electric scheme, which commenced operations in 1929.*

nGaedheal pro-treaty tradition. There was therefore an apparent irony in the fact that it was Costello's government which enacted legislation declaring an Irish republic. The 1948 Republic of Ireland Act led to the formal inauguration of a republic in April 1949. Thirty-three years after the Easter Rebellion, therefore, a republic was established in Ireland. But it was established by a government whose largest participant – Fine Gael – had grown from the side that had *beaten* the republicans in the 1922-23 civil war. In fact the irony was more apparent than substantial. Certainly the 1948 act brought Irish unity no nearer to realisation. This was underlined by the passing at Westminster of the 1949 Ireland Act which stated that no part of Northern Ireland would leave the United Kingdom without the consent of the Northern Ireland parliament. The south might be called a republic, but the all-Ireland republican dream was still well beyond reach.

In 1959 the man who had for many been a symbol of the republic – Eamon de Valera – was elected to the presidency and Sean Lemass took over as Taoiseach. Lemass had lengthy political experience,

Belfast). The vibrant local cultures did coexist. But tension was a persistent motif.

James Craig (who had been involved in pre-partition unionist politics) had become Northern Ireland's first prime minister in 1921. He remained in this position until his death in 1940. He was succeeded by J.M. Andrews. Then in 1943 Basil Brooke assumed office and retained the premiership until 1963. In that year Terence O'Neill became Northern Ireland's prime minister, and it was his period in office which witnessed the ugly eruption of the continuing violence within the northern state. In 1967 the Northern Ireland Civil Rights Association was set up to redress grievance. Demands were met with mixed responses, including that of violence. The late-1960s saw the reappearance of bloody, tribal fighting with the British army called in during 1969 to part the waves of sectarian hostility. In 1972 the Stormont parliament and government were suspended, with direct rule from Westminster being imposed. Over the subsequent years violence and sectarian polarisation have gained most of the headlines emanating from the region. A variety of initiatives have failed to dent the stalemate, the 1985 Anglo-Irish agreement between the British and southern Irish governments being the most significant recent example. But the geographical and social variations of experience within Northern Ireland are enormous. And while this helps provide no obvious solutions it ought, perhaps, to influence the thinking of those who pursue them.

Yet solutions remain elusive in the Northern Irish conflict. Throughout much of Irish history the themes which have generated fascination have been precisely those which have resulted in mutual hostility. The existence of competing, self-sustaining forces in Ireland has in many instances culminated in conflict. The colour and complexity of overlapping cultures has rendered the island's history both compelling and painful. Irish history has witnessed inconclusive attempts at domination by one or more groups over others. Waves of invasion, patterns of settlement, religious and ethnic identity and difference – these have repeatedly been the motive forces of Irish historical experience.

Such forces represent addictive substances for the historian. But it is also true that they have helped to produce an island rich in appeal for many other people as well. The history of Ireland is alive and visible in a wide range of forms. Many of the pictures included in these pages bear witness to the accessibility of the past as embodied in a fertile and varied present. Architecture, artefact and land; ritual and religious expression; musical, literary, and sporting cultures – each testifies to the vibrant past which is discernible in Ireland's present.

Above: *Eamon de Valera, in the light coat and glasses, among the pilgrims ascending Croagh Patrick, County Mayo, in 1932.*

Far left: *Douglas Hyde in 1938, after being inaugurated as Eire's first president. Second from the left is Eamon de Valera.*

Overleaf: *children bringing home the turf, Glenariff, 1954.*

having been influentially involved in Fianna Fail since its inception. Having promoted protection of domestic industry as a Fianna Fail minister in the 1930s, Lemass shifted ground, now pushing for foreign investment in Ireland and for freer trade. One manifestation of the latter was the signing in 1965 of the Anglo-Irish Free Trade Agreement (which provided Irish industry with immediate tariff-free access to the British market). In the same year Lemass met the Northern Ireland prime minister , Terence O'Neill, in Belfast and in Dublin. But prime ministerial cross-border gestures proved not to be prophetic and the painful contradiction of the northeast of Ireland were soon to explode into tragedy.

Within Northern Ireland a majority-leaning state had been maintained. Whatever discrimination occurred was directed against the Catholic minority. Sectarian tension and sectarian violence are not recent developments in the northeast of Ireland, though their more recent forms have taken distinctive and particular forms. The political dominance of the unionist tradition was firmly rooted in the Northern Irish parliament at Stormont (on the outskirts of

Left: *milking, 1952.*

Right: *gathering kelp in County Clare, during the 1930s.*

Below: *turf cutting, 1915.*

These pages: *traditional cottages, single-storied and brightened with whitewash, their roofs thatched using local materials.*

Above: *bonding wheels at Caloghane in County Kerry.*

Left: *near Kinvara, County Clare. Flann O'Brien said "a good bicycle is a geat companion, there is a great charm about it".*

Right: *"Blarney Street, Cork City".*

Left: *a Dublin street market in the mid-1940s.*

Right: *early 1940s economic encouragement!*

Below: *the 26th Battalion lined up on the parade ground in the 1940s. Ireland's neutrality in World War Two involved some tense moments with belligerent nations.*

IN YOUR OWN
and the
NATION'S
INTEREST

PLOUGH MORE LAND

AND PRODUCE MORE FOOD

Left: *Croagh Patrick pilgrims, County Mayo. Religious conviction and practice remain crucial factors in many people's lives in modern Ireland.*

Above: *Croagh Patrick, County Mayo. According to legend, St. Patrick spent forty days here praying and fasting.*

Below: *pilgrims on the arduous climb up Croagh Patrick's scree-covered slopes.*

Above: *declaration ceremony for the Republic of Ireland, 1949. President Sean T. O'Kelly and Mrs. O'Kelly are on the stand.*

Left: *removal of the statue of Queen Victoria from outside Leinster House, seat of the Dail (or parliament) in Dublin.*

Above right: *demonstration by the unemployed in 1953; tragically, unemployment has remained an all-too-persistent feature of modern Irish experience.*

Right: *an appealing feature of modern Irish experience: traditional music in a traditional context.*

Dublin old and new. The ornate ironwork of the St. Stephen's Green Centre (left) echoes that of the balconies along elegant Fitzwilliam Square (right).

Above: *a Guinness barge chugging past the Four Courts building, Dublin, 1950.*

Left: *Dublin bus station, designed by Michael Scott and finished in the early 1950s.*

Right: *the Powerscourt Townhouse development, South William Street, Dublin. Built in 1771 by Robert Mack for Viscount Powerscourt, Powerscourt House was later occupied by a wholesale textile firm before being converted into a shopping centre in the 1980s.*

Above: *the north bank of the River Lee and the tower of St. Anne's Shandon (1722), Cork City.*

Right: *the west door of nineteenth-century St. Finbarr's Cathedral, Cork.*

Left: *a golden sunset over Cork.*

Overleaf: *Iris Meain, Aran Islands, County Galway.*

Previous pages: *Aras an Uachtarain, Phoenix Park, official residence of the President of Ireland since 1937.*

Left: *Leinster House, once home of the Duke of Leinster, now houses the Irish Parliament. The obelisk commemorates patriots Michael Collins and Arthur Griffith.*

Left: *Dublin's O'Connell Street and the O'Connell Monument.*

Above: *the Bank of Ireland. Formerly the Irish Parliament House, the building's use changed with the Act of Union and the abolition of the Irish Parliament.*

Above: *the statue of George Bernard Shaw (1856-1950) outside the National Gallery of Ireland.*

Right: *the General Post Office, historic headquarters of the 1916 Rising and the birthplace of independent Ireland.*

Left: *the entrance to Kilmainham Jail. Incarcerated within its walls were many political prisoners, and it was here that the leaders of the 1916 Rising were executed.*

Right: *restored and opened as a museum in 1966, Kilmainham Jail houses exhibits relating to Ireland's struggle for independence.*

Right: *the stark cells of Kilmainham jail.*

Left: *Belfast Castle. Completed in 1870, the castle overlooks the city from a site 400 feet above sea level on the slopes of Cave Hill.*

Right: *Belfast City Hall. The city's central feature, it was built in the Renaissance style between 1898 and 1906.*

Below left: *the parliament buildings, Stormont, Belfast. Northern Ireland's Stormont government was replaced in 1972 by direct rule from London.*

Below right: *an old photograph of Queen's University, Belfast; the nineteenth-century building was designed by Charles Lanyon.*

Overleaf: *Belfast City Hall, impressively lit at night.*

Above: *William T. Cosgrave (1880-1965). As President of the Executive Council, Cosgrave led the Cumann na n Gaedheal Free State government (1922-32).*

Below: *President John F. Kennedy with Eamon de Valera, Dublin, 1963.*

Above: *Eamon de Valera greeting the Papal Legate, Cardinal Agagianian, in 1961.*

Below: *Alfred Chester Beatty receiving a degree at the N.U.I. from Eamon de Valera, 1951.*

Above: *Sean Lemass, who succeeded de Valera as Fianna Fail leader and Taoiseach (prime minister) in 1959. He died in 1971.*

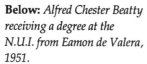

Above: *Archbishop McQuaid in 1961, with Eamon Andrews (left), Chairman, and Edward Roth (centre), Director General of R.T.E.*

Below right: *shooting* The Quiet Man, *starring John Wayne and Maureen O'Hara, in 1951.*

Right: *Samuel Beckett (1906-89), Irish novelist and dramatist concerned with the basic problems and anguish of the human condition.*

Above: *Dublin's River Liffey and the green-domed Custom House. The building's interior was destroyed during fighting in 1921, but has since been restored.*

Above: *the Mansion House, site of the first meeting of the Dail Eireann in 1919, and of the signing of the truce in 1921.*

Left: *Charles Haughey, Fianna Fail leader, in 1986.*

Far left below: *the Republic's Garret FitzGerald and the U.K.'s Margaret Thatcher at the signing of the 1985 Anglo-Irish Agreement.*

Below left: *Terence O'Neill (left) and Jack Lynch (right). O'Neill was Northern Irish Prime Minister, 1963-9; Lynch replaced Lemass as Taoiseach in 1966.*

Right: *Ronald Regan and Garret FitzGerald at Shannon Airport in 1984.*

Below: *drinking in presidential surroundings!*

Left: *fomer President of the Republic of Ireland, Dr. Hillery.*

Below left: *Charles Haughey, Fianna Fail leader and several times the Republic's Taoiseach.*

Below: *first female President of the Republic, Mary Robinson.*

Left: *the then President of the U.S.A., Ronald Regan, in Ireland in 1984.*

Below left: *John Hume, born in Derry in 1937, and leader of the Social Democratic and Labour Party since 1979.*

Below: *Garret FitzGerald, born in 1926 in Dublin, and leader of Fine Gael from 1977 to 1987. FitzGerald was Taoiseach in 1981/82 and from 1982 to 1987.*

Above: *1979 anti-abortion march. Abortion is illegal and constitutionally prohibited in the Republic of Ireland.*

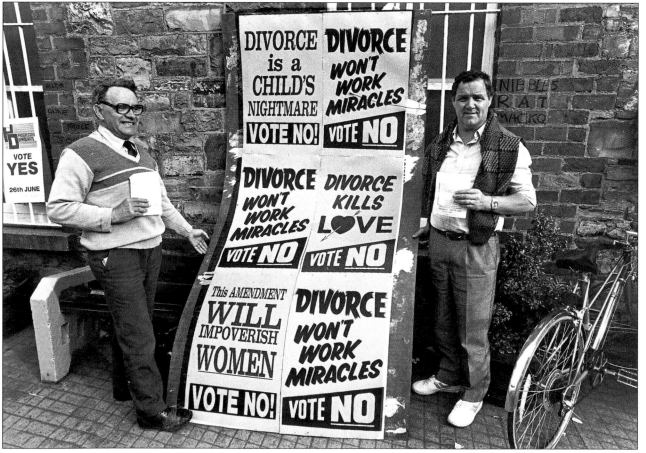

Left: *1984 Dublin march organised by the Irish Campaign against Reagan's Foreign Policy because of Reagan's visit to Ireland.*

Right: *Nell McCafferty, writer, born in 1944.*

Below left: *outside a polling station in the 1986 divorce referendum in the Republic; the campaign to delete the constitutional prohibition on divorce was defeated.*

Below: *a 1983 march in Dublin opposing the proposed amendment to the constitution, explicitly to prohibit abortion; the amendment was carried by referendum.*

POLITICAL PRISONER
LONG KESH
ONE OF MANY MEN ALMOST BEATEN TO DEATH BY BRITISH TROOPS
AFTER THE BURNING OF LONG KESH CONCENTRATION CAMPS ON THE
15th OCTOBER, 1974.
Issued by Belfast Sinn Fein

Above and above left:
*demonstrators on Belfast's
Falls Road supporting the
plight of republican prisoners
in the notorious H-Block, in
1980.*

Left: *Sinn Fein Conference,
1986.*

Right: *IRA gunman.*

Left: *riots during republican hunger strikes; such strikes have been a recurring phenomenon in modern Irish republican experience.*

Right: *another recurring theme – militaristic gestures. IRA gunmen fire a volley in honour of a dead colleague.*

Below: *young blood. IRA graffiti in the 1970s calls for recruits in Belfast.*

Below: *Bernadette McAliskey, a leader of the 1960s civil rights movement, at a 1981 press conference, after an attempt on her life.*

Right: *the funeral of an IRA hunger striker.*

Left: *British soldiers on duty in Northern Ireland.*

Above: *Ian Paisley, who founded the Democractic Unionist Party in 1971.*

Below: *masked loyalists in front of an Ulster Defence Association mural.*

Above: *UDA members march through the streets of Belfast in 1972.*

Left: *Ulster Volunteer Force gunmen at a press conference.*

Right: *"Ulster says no" to the Anglo-Irish Agreement. Loyalists protest against the Agreement, signed in 1985 by the British and Irish governments.*

Above: *Ian Paisley pictured with a sledgehammer during the 1985 "Smash Sinn Fein" campaign, prior to the local council elections.*

Right: *unionists burning an effigy of Margaret Thatcher, in protest at her signing of the 1985 Anglo-Irish Agreement.*

Left: *Eamon Coughlan during the 5,000m final at the Seoul Olympics in 1988.*

Above: *Clannad, Irish folk/ rock group, in concert.*

Above right: *the actor, Cyril Cusack, pictured in 1985.*

Right: *modern Irish folk singer, Christy Moore.*

Above: *writers Ulick O'Connor (left) and Christy Brown.*

Above left: *major Irish contemporary artist, Louis le Brocquy.*

Left: *actress Siobhan McKenna.*

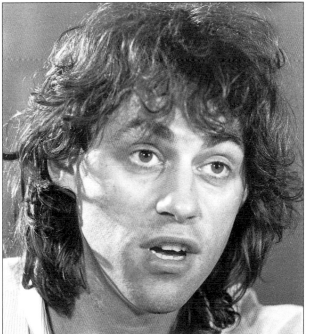

Above: *Irish singer-songwriter Van Morrison pictured with Bob Dylan at a concert in 1984.*

Left: *Bob Geldof pictured in 1985, the year of his celebrated Live Aid project.*

Right: *Seamus Heaney, one of Ireland's best-known contemporary poets.*

CHRONOLOGY

521/522	Birth of Colum Cille
563	Colum Cille moved to Iona
597	Death of Colum Cille
7th century	*Book of Durrow*
8th century	*Book of Kells*
795	Viking raid on Iona
1014	Battle of Clontarf
1152	Synod of Kells
1169	First significant Norman contingent arrived in Ireland
1170	Strongbow arrived in Ireland
1171	Henry II arrived in Ireland
1183	Gerald of Wales' first visit to Ireland
1315	Edward Bruce invaded Ireland
1366	Statutes of Kilkenny

Above: *Drombeg Stone Circle, Glandore, West Cork.*

Left: *the keep and reinforced outer walls of Cahir Castle, County Tipperary.*

Right: *the twelfth-century round tower of St. Brigid's, Kildare, probably one of the last to be built in Ireland.*

1494	Poynings' parliament met
1534	Outbreak of Lord Offaly's rebellion
1541	Irish parliament confirmed Henry VIII as King of Ireland
1585	Hugh O'Neill became Earl of Tyrone
1598	Battle of the Yellow Ford
1601	Battle of Kinsale
1607	Flight of the earls
1609	Articles of Plantation
1641	Outbreak of rebellion
1649	Massacres at Drogheda and Wexford
1662	Act of Settlement
1689	James II landed in Ireland
1690	William III landed in Ireland

Above: *Cork City.*

1690	Battle of the Boyne
1719	Toleration Act
1720	Declaratory Act
1724	Swift's *Drapier's Letters*
1782	Declaratory Act repealed
1798	Outbreaks of rebellion
1800	Act of Union
1803	Emmet's rebellion
1823	Catholic Association founded
1829	Catholic Emancipation Act
1842	*Nation* first published

1845-9	Famine
1848	William Smith O'Brien's rising
1858	Establishment of the Irish Republican Brotherhood
1867	Fenian rising
1870	Foundation of the Home Government Association
1879	Foundation of the Irish National Land League
1884	Foundation of the Gaelic Athletic Association
1886	First Home Rule Bill
1891	Death of Parnell
1893	Second Home Rule Bill
1903	Wyndham Act
1912	Third Home Rule Bill
1912	Solemn League and Covenant signed
1913	Foundation of Ulster Volunteer Force and of Irish Volunteers
1916	Easter rebellion
1919-21	Anglo-Irish war
1921	Anglo-Irish 'treaty'
1922-3	Civil war
1932	Fianna Fail first came to power
1937	De Valera's constitution
1948	Republic of Ireland Act
1949	Ireland Act
1956-62	Border campaign by Irish Republican Army
1967	Northern Ireland Civil Rights Association founded
1972	Imposition of direct rule on Northern Ireland
1985	Anglo-Irish Agreement

Above: *Georgian door, Dublin.*

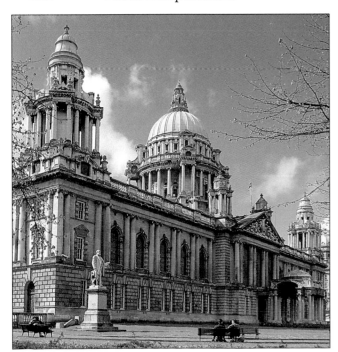

Left: *Belfast City Hall.*

Right: *British soldiers in Northern Ireland.*

ℬIBLIOGRAPHY

For those who would like to pursue further reading on Irish history, the following are recommended:

M. Richter, *Medieval Ireland: The Enduring Tradition* (Dublin, Gill and Macmillan, 1988)

R.F. Foster, *Modern Ireland 1600-1972* (London, Allen Lane, 1988)

D.G. Boyce, *Nineteenth-Century Ireland: The Search for Stability* (Dublin, Gill and Macmillan, 1990)

J.J. Lee, *Ireland 1912-1985: Politics and Society* (Cambridge, Cambridge University Press, 1989).